OVER THE RIVER...
LIFE OF LYDIA MARIA CHILD
ABOLITIONIST FOR FREEDOM
1802-1880

A COMPANION BOOK TO THE EPIC DOCUMENTARY
OF THE SAME NAME

DISCOVER AMERICA'S
TURMOIL OF THE 1800s

WITHDRAWN

PERMANENT PRODUCTIONS PUBLISHING

OVER THE RIVER...
LIFE OF LYDIA MARIA CHILD
ABOLITIONIST FOR FREEDOM
1802-1880

A COMPANION BOOK TO THE EPIC DOCUMENTARY
OF THE SAME NAME

DISCOVER AMERICA'S
TURMOIL OF THE 1800s

Constance L. Jackson

Introduction by Carolyn L. Karcher, Ph.D.

Printing: Delta Printing Solutions, Valencia CA

Copyright 2008 by Constance L. Jackson
Published by Permanent Productions, Inc.
904 Silver Spur Rd., R.H.E., CA 90274
www.permproductions.com
Rolling Hills Estates, CA

All Rights Reserved. No part of this publication may be reproduced, stored in a retrieval system, or transmitted in any form by any means, electronic, mechanical, photocopying, recording, or otherwise, without the prior permission of Permanent Productions, Inc.

The paper in this book meets the minimum requirements of the American National Standard for Permanence of Paper for Printed Library Material. The binding materials have been chosen for strength and durability.

Library of Congress Cataloging-in-Publication Data

Jackson, Constance L. (Constance Lillie), 1954-
    Over the river-- : life of Lydia Maria Child, abolitionist for freedom, 1802-1880 : a companion book to the epic documentary of the same name / Constance L. Jackson ; introduction by Carolyn L. Karcher.
      p. cm.
    Summary: "A biography of a popular writer who, in the mid-19th century, supported the immediate abolition of slavery, which caused adverse public response that catapulted her into advocating for African-American rights, for women's rights, and for better treatment of Native Americans"--Provided by publisher.
    Includes bibliographical references and index.
    ISBN 978-0-9818204-0-8 (pbk. : alk. paper)
    1. Child, Mrs. (Lydia Maria), 1802-1880--Juvenile literature. 2. Women social reformers--United States--Biography--Juvenile literature. 3. Women abolitionists--United States--Biography--Juvenile literature. 4. Authors, American--19th century--Biography--Juvenile literature. 5. Antislavery movements--United States--History--19th century--Juvenile literature. 6. African Americans--Social conditions--19th century--Juvenile literature 7. Social justice--United States--History--19th century--Juvenile literature. I. Title.
HQ1413.C45J33 2008
326'.8092--dc22
[B]
                              2008023790

Manufactured in the United States of America on acid-free paper

Bookcover Designed by: Constance L. Jackson
Graphic Artist: David Loredo
Book Interior Design: Patricia Rasch
Book Indexing: Clive Pyne

On the cover: Lydia Maria Child in 1856, top left-David Child, lower left-William Lloyd Garrison, left top and right center—actor James Moses Black, lower right corner, 5 Generations of a slave family, anti-slavery poster, bottom books written by Lydia Maria Child.

Backcover: Civil War Illustration (Library of Congress)

Frontispiece: Lydia Maria Francis in 1826, the year she first published the *Juvenile Miscellany*

In Loving Memory

In loving memory of my mom, Willie Mae Gordon-Jackson, who despite her deafness and after a bitter divorce when I was 11 months old, raised me along with my seven siblings single-handedly. After many years of home study courses to obtain her high school diploma, then continuing higher education in business, my mother was an excellent role model, even after her death, when I was just 20-years-old. She is credited for fostering my thirst for knowledge, my interest in business, and my appreciation of cultural diversity.

And

In loving memory of Michael and Dorothy Patterson, who encouraged their daughter Michele to embrace diversity and to achieve despite the obstacles. And two people that I hold dear to my heart.

Table of Contents

A Few Words xi

Introduction by Carolyn L. Karcher, Ph.D. xiii

Books and literary works
written by Lydia Maria Child xx

Story Preface by Historians xxv

Chapter One 1
Heritage

Chapter Two 11
Maria's Fictional Stories:
Hobomok, Juvenile Miscellany, Evenings in New England, The Rebels, and *The Juvenile Miscellany* Children's Magazine

    True Love: David and Maria

Chapter Three 17
Slavery And Democracy:
The Great Cotton Conflict

    A Relationship Made In Heaven?

    Maria's Domestic Advice Book and David's Debts:
    The Frugal Housewife,

    The Mother's Book, and *The Little Girl's Own Book*

    The Beginning of the End to Slavery: Black Civil Rights and Women's Rights

    Brewing Insurrection in Virginia

    Abolitionism, Unionism, State Rights, and Jacksonian Politics

    Maria's Anguish over David / Garrison Hails Maria "The First Woman in the Republic"

    Garrisonians

    Maria's Literary Bombshell and the Personal Attacks Against Her

    Maria Blames Herself for David's Impractical Business Schemes/1835 "The Year of the Mob"

    Maria Supports David's Beet Farming Project

    Maria's Transcendental Loves

    Maria Creates a New Style of Writing called Essays or Sketches

Chapter Four 53
More Congressional Infighting/Moral Repulsion Of Slavery & Maria's Deep Depression

    Maria Publishes a Pioneering First:
    The Progress of Religious Ideas

    Moral Repulsion Over the Spread of Slavery into the West

    "Free Soil ! Free Speech !, Free Men ! Fremont!"

Chapter Five... 65
Secession Looming/John Brown's Raid/Maria's Resurgence

    Aging Maria Continues Her Push to Abolish Slavery/ Secession & Civil War Looming

    Maria Writes *The Freedmen's Book*

    The Fight to Abolish Slavery has Ended

Chapter Six.. 77
A New Day for America?/Reconstruction Policy— First Civil Rights Bill Passed in 1866

    Rest in Peace, Maria

Acknowledgements 83

Illustrations Credits... 85

Books About Lydia Maria Child 87

Index 88

PERMANENT PRODUCTIONS PUBLISHING

This book, *Over the River... Life of Lydia Maria Child, Abolitionist for Freedom*, a companion version of the epic documentary, is a rich description of Child's major literary participation in changing the social conditions during the 19th-century, highlighting issues that were and are still very relevant today. Few Americans realize that the struggle to end slavery in America actually started over 50 years before the *Emancipation Proclamation* by folks called abolitionists.

Narrated by the well-regarded actress, Diahann Carroll, the DVD of *Over the River...* brings Child's America to life with re-enactments, rarely seen photographs, paintings, political cartoons, and other visual images that add another dimension to her story. To purchase the DVD, please go to **www.overtherivermovie.com** or find it at major bookstores or libraries.

Young Lydia Maria Child

Author's Note

Constance L. Jackson,
Writer, Producer, Director

As the writer, director, and producer of the documentary, I was drawn to Lydia Maria Child because she was the first female in American history, that I knew of, black or white, who dedicated her whole adult life to abolish slavery and to advocate for social change. Today, her acts are seen as being noble, but during her time, they were considered radical. Not only was Lydia Maria Child an advocate for abolishing slavery, but she was also quite ahead of her time in sharing through her literary works, the importance of people loving one another, caring about the sufferings of others, and doing something about it.

I wondered after extensively researching her life, if I had met up to the ideals she espoused, and how could I, in my small way, help foster others to live up to those ideals? I decided that making an important epic documentary featuring the important players—black and white, who worked tirelessly together, risking their lives for our freedom was a major contribution.

To make sure that the world recognized Lydia Maria Child's valuable presence in bringing about a better America, I was also instrumental in obtaining her nomination and subsequent posthumous induction into the National Women's Hall of Fame in Seneca Falls, New York in 2001. She is also an inductee at the National Abolition Hall of Fame in Peterboro, New York.

The reader can also visit the following museums and historical societies that highlight Mrs. Child's life: The Wayland Historical Society, Wayland, MA (has artifacts and tours), Sturbridge Village, Sturbridge, MA (has cookbooks, literature written by her, and foods prepared in their restaurant from Child's *Frugal Housewife*); Genesee Country Village & Museum (has a Lydia Maria Child re-enactor talking with visitors at the village, and they also sell books by Lydia Maria Child).

A Few Words

by Michele Patterson, Esq., Executive Producer of the DVD

I have always been fascinated with history. As a child, Abraham Lincoln was my hero. My goal was to read every single book about him in the children's section of the library.

As I grew older, I began noticing that something was missing both in school and in the bookstores. Where were the women, the people of color, anyone other than white men? Certainly they existed in years past. Were there no female heroes, no reason to celebrate the accomplishments of these Americans?

Lydia Maria Child is one of those heroes who were nearly forgotten, but for her Thanksgiving Day poem turned song, *Over the River and through the Woods to Grandmother's House We Go*. Was it because she was a woman? Was it because she fought with words rather than guns? Was it because she crusaded for Indian rights, African-Americans rights, prison reform, or religious tolerance? Was it perhaps because she had no children to continue her legacy? The reason may be all of these. *Over the River... Life of Lydia Maria Child, Abolitionist for Freedom* helps to broaden our understanding of American history by bringing this patriot to life and sharing the complexities and some of the social conflicts of the nineteenth century.

History should be more than just learning about presidents and wars. It should also be about exploring our past so that we can better understand the struggles that plague us today. In making *Over the River...*, we hope to interest more Americans to learn about our heritage by including more women and people of color in the experience. Discovering Lydia Maria Child, and sharing the fullness of her life, is a terrific way to begin, since she was so central to reforming America. If her literary works about racial harmony and women's rights had been embraced sooner, perhaps our social conditions would not be so pandemic.

Introduction

**By Carolyn L. Karcher, Ph.D.,
lead biographer of Lydia Maria Child**

Constance Jackson's magnificent documentary *Over the River...Life of Lydia Maria Child, Abolitionist for Freedom* restores to a wide audience a true American hero–a woman whose courageous struggle to make her country fulfill its ideals of democracy, justice, and equality still teaches valuable lessons today. Born in 1802, the daughter of a hard-working baker in Medford, Massachusetts, Lydia Francis (who had herself rebaptized Maria in 1821) grew up before colleges for women existed, but she did not let restricted opportunities prevent her from educating herself. She also learned at a youthful age to identify with other groups excluded from the "inalienable rights" America's founding creed promised to "all men."

The first such group to awaken young Lydia's sympathies were the Abenaki Indians she encountered in Maine, where she lived for six years after her mother's death (1815-21). Driven off their land and reduced to destitution, yet blamed for their own plight by the very white settlers who occupied their territory, the Abenakis opened Lydia's eyes to her country's plundering of the Indians. She would agitate for a fair and humane Indian

xiii

policy throughout her life, beginning in 1829 with her protest against the forced "removal" of the Cherokees from their native Georgia to Oklahoma–a protest she carried on jointly with her newly-wed husband David Lee Child–and ending in 1870 with her outraged denunciation of the brutal war being waged on the Plains Indians.

Championship of the Indians led Lydia Maria Child naturally to the crusade against slavery and racism that became her greatest contribution to transforming US history. Sought out in 1830 by the radical abolitionist William Lloyd Garrison, who admired her writings and wanted her to dedicate her literary talents to the antislavery cause, Child undertook the research that bore fruit in her *Appeal in Favor of That Class of Americans Called Africans* (1833), the abolitionist movement's earliest full-scale analysis of the slavery question, an analysis never surpassed in comprehensiveness. The book's eight chapters examined the institution of slavery from every angle–historical, legal, economic, political, racial, and moral.

Looking beyond slavery to the imperative of incorporating African Americans into US society as equal citizens, Child also refuted the myth of African inferiority, condemned racial prejudice as incompatible with American values, and called for abolishing all forms of discrimination, whether in jobs, schools, public facilities, civil rights, or laws against interracial marriage. The *Appeal*'s ambitious scope, meticulous thoroughness, intellectual depth, and rhetorical power won it enormous influence as an antislavery tract and enduring renown as a work of pioneering historical scholarship. It recruited into abolitionist ranks a formidable array of opinion makers and future political leaders, emboldened women to assume public roles in a bitter political controversy, and encouraged literary figures who had been keeping aloof from abolitionists to join them in speaking and writing against slavery.

The commitment to eradicating racism that Child expressed in the *Appeal* and acted on in her life inspired African Americans as well, giving them hope that an alliance with progressive whites could overcome obstacles to equality. In the segregated world of nineteenth-century America, the abolitionist movement provided the first forum in which African and European Americans could mingle socially and work together toward a common goal, and Child played an instrumental part in breaking down racial barriers both within and outside that forum.

Challenging white Americans' prejudices cost Child a flourishing literary career, along with the social standing she had gained through it. When she published the *Appeal,* she stood at the apex of the literary popularity she had earned by producing works that filled broadly recognized cultural needs: two novels illuminating aspects of colonial history and thus helping to create a distinctively American literature, *Hobomok, a Tale of Early Times* (1824) and *The Rebels,* or *Boston before the Revolution* (1825); a children's magazine that molded a generation of New England youth, the *Juvenile Miscellany* (1826-34); a pair of best-selling domestic advice books oriented toward women of modest means, *The Frugal Housewife* (1829) and *The Mother's Book* (1831); and a series of women's biographies that offered readers a range of role models suitable for an era of social change.

In tackling the explosive issues of slavery and racism, Child was filling an even more urgent cultural need, but this time her hitherto adoring audience reacted with fury. A prominent Massachusetts politician hurled the *Appeal* out of the window with a pair of fire tongs, the Boston Athenaeum rescinded her free library privileges, former patrons slammed their doors in her face, readers boycotted her books, parents cancelled their subscriptions to her children's magazine, publishers rejected her manuscripts, and Child lost her sole source of revenue. Yet she never looked back.

Over a career of advocacy that lasted until her death in 1880, Child published countless other works promoting racial justice and equality–tracts, biographies, newspaper articles, letters to politicians, stories, a novel presenting intermarriage as the solution to America's race problem (*A Romance of the Republic*, 1867), and a primer for the emancipated slaves featuring readings by and about people of African descent (*The Freedmen's Book*, 1865). In addition, she edited a major abolitionist newspaper, the *National Anti-Slavery Standard* (1841-43), and a slave narrative now considered a literary classic, Harriet Jacobs's *Incidents in the Life of a Slave Girl* (1861). While polishing Jacobs's manuscript and maximizing its sales, moreover, Child forged a warm friendship with its author that lasted into the Reconstruction era. She and Jacobs collaborated in raising the consciousness of white northerners, publicizing the heroism African American troops displayed during the Civil War, advancing the education of the former slaves, agitating for the distribution of plantation land to the freed people, and campaigning for Black Suffrage.

Child's prodigious record as an activist for racial equality represents only part of her legacy, however. Like many abolitionist women, Child confronted severe restraints on her own freedom as she militated for the freedom of the slaves. This issue began engaging her as early as 1835, when she published a two-volume *History of the Condition of Women* that ranged from ancient to modern times and covered every known culture. By the 1840s, Child was writing angry articles attacking the double standard and exposing the fallacy of claims that the liberation of women would destroy feminine delicacy. She was also writing stories that covertly celebrated women's sexuality. After the Civil War, Child turned toward formulating cogent arguments for woman suffrage. Simultaneously, she censured those feminist leaders who pitted white women against African American men in a competitive quest for enfranchisement.

Many of the other causes Child embraced likewise resonate strongly for our own time. Her lifelong search for a religion that could satisfy her spiritual hunger, social conscience, and rational mind impelled her to combat doctrinal bigotry and sectarianism and to plead for religious tolerance. At a time when even many liberals considered it heretical to deny the status of Christianity as the only true faith, Child longed to "become acquainted with some good, intelligent Brahmin, or Mohammedan," so that she could "learn, in some degree, how their religions appeared to *them*." She fulfilled that dream vicariously through research that culminated in two major works: a three-volume comparative study setting Hinduism, Buddhism, Jainism, Confucianism, Taoism, Zoroastrianism, Judaism, Christianity, and Islam on an equal footing, *The Progress of Religious Ideas, Through Successive Ages* (1855); and an anthology of extracts from the sacred texts of these and other religions of the ancient and modern worlds, *Aspirations of the World. A Chain of Opals* (1878).

Of Child's vast body of writings, the ones twenty-first century readers may find most relevant to our society's persistent social problems are her articles on urban poverty, immigration, the prison system, and capital punishment. Child began addressing these issues in the 1840s, when she moved to New York to edit the *National Anti-Slavery Standard*. New York then teemed with desperately poor European immigrants, who often subsisted on hawking, begging, and prostitution; slept on the pavements; and crowded the prisons. Child movingly described their plight in her weekly column for the *Standard*, "Letters from New-York," placed alongside her editorials on slavery. The juxtaposition invited readers to extend their sympathies from African Americans to Irish, Italian, and Jewish immigrants and to connect southern slavery with the forms of oppression that prevailed in the North.

Child's vignettes of ragged urchins "fighting furiously" for pennies, emaciated mothers and children with "hungry eyes," drunken paupers lying in the gutter, and homeless women harassed by the police put a human face on poverty. "If we can abolish *poverty*, we shall have taken the greatest step towards the abolition of *crime*," Child argued. Building "penitentiaries and prisons" did not help, she insisted, for the "whole system tended to *increase* crime." Child also condemned capital punishment as "legalized murder," warning against "the danger of convicting the innocent."

These words sound timelier than ever as economic policies drive more and more people into poverty, homeless indigents swamp our cities, descendants of European immigrants persecute a new generation of immigrants from Latin America, the US incarcerates more prisoners than any other country in the world, capital punishment still victimizes innocents as well as criminals (though it has been abolished in all western democracies except our own), and only China, Iran, Saudi Arabia, and Pakistan exceed the US in the number of executions.

A century and a quarter after Child's death, her legacy remains vital to those who share her vision of a society in which people of all races, religions, and national origins can live harmoniously together as equals. The interracial solidarity that she and her abolitionist comrades modeled achieved the overthrow of slavery and the passage of the 14th and 15th Amendments, but the racial equality for which they and their successors in the 1960s' Civil Rights movement fought has not yet been completely attained. Nor has the even thornier problem of justice for America's dispossessed Indians come close to resolution. Women have made enormous strides since Child's day, but they continue to face some of the difficulties she contended with in her life and wrote about in her fiction and journalism: sexist stereotypes, double standards, unequal marriages, economic barriers, sexual exploitation and violence.

Despite the diffusion of secularism—or perhaps in reaction against it—our era has seen a worldwide resurgence of fundamentalism and religious warfare that makes Child's call for tolerance as urgent now as in her time. Amid the looming challenges of the future, Child's self-sacrificing life, her courage in braving public ostracism to stand up for her principles, and her brilliant insights into the dynamics of slavery, racism, sexism, religious bigotry, poverty, crime, and punishment will inspire activists to continue the struggle for a better world.

Books and literary works written by Lydia Maria Child

1824 *Hobomok; Evenings in New England*

1825 *The Rebels*

1826 *Juvenile Miscellany* Magazine for Children, "The Rival Brothers" (first Short Story)

1827 *Emily Parker*; *The Juvenile Souvenir*; and "The Lone Indian" (short story for *The Token*)

1828 "The Indian Wife," *The Church in the Wilderness, Moral Lessons in Verse, Biographical Sketches of Great and Good Men*

1829 *The First Settlers of New England*

"Chocorua's Curse"

"Comparative Strength of Male and Female Intellect" and other articles in the *Massachusetts Journal* Newspaper

The Frugal Housewife

1830 "St. Domingo Orphans" (first anti-slavery short story in the *Juvenile Miscellany*)

1831 *The Little Girl's Own Book*

"Jumbo and Zairee" (second anti-slavery short story in the *Juvenile Miscellany*)

The Mother's Book

Writes editorials against racial prejudice in the *Massachusetts Journal*

1832 *The Biographies of Madame de Stael, Madame Roland, Lady Russell,* and *Madame Guyon*

Books and literary works written by Lydia Maria Child

1833 *An Appeal In Favor of that Class of Americans Called Africans*

1834 *Oasis* (anti-slavery gift book)

1835 *History of the Condition of Women, Authentic Anecdotes of American Slavery* (pamphlet)

1836 *The Evils of Slavery, The Cure of Slavery, Anti-Slavery Catechism* (pamphlets)

Philothea (Transcendental book)

1837 *The Family Nurse*

1839 "Charity Bowery" (inaugural issue of the *Liberty Bell*)

1840 "The Black Saxons" (story in the *Liberty Bell*)

1841 Editor of the *National Anti Slavery Standard* (NASS) newspaper

"Letters from New York" (essays or sketches) in the *National Anti-Slavery Standard*

"The Quadroons" (story in the *Liberty Bell*)

1842 "Slavery's Pleasant Home" (story in the *Liberty Bell*)

1843 *Letters from New York* (book of compiled essays from the NASS)

1847-1847 Within a few years she published Three Volumes of *Flowers for Children* and multiple articles and stories for various magazines.

1853 *Isaac T. Hopper: A True Life*

1855 *Progress of Religious Ideas* (book); *A New Flower for Children*; and "Jan and Zaida" (story in the *Liberty Bell*)

1856 Multiple articles and stories for various publications: "The Kansas Imigrants" (in *New York Tribune*), writes "Song for the Free Soil Men," and *Autumnal Leaves*

1860 Publishes *Correspondence between Lydia Maria Child and Gov. Wise and Mrs. Mason,* edits Harriet Jacobs's *Incidents in the Life of a Slave Girl.* Publishes pamphlets including *The Duty of Disobedience to the Fugitive Slave Law*

1865-1865 Publishes various articles and writes to President Lincoln in 1862. *Looking Toward Sunset* (an anthology of positive views of old age). *The Freedmen's Book*

1867 A Romance of the Republic

1868-1870 Publishes "A Plea for the Indian" and *An Appeal for the Indians.* Writes many articles over the next couple of years for the *Standard, Woman's Advocate, Woman's Journal, and Independent,* imploring black suffrage, including land redistribution, women's suffrage, and Indian rights. "Resemblance between the Buddhist and Catholic Religions" in the *The Atlantic Monthly.*

1878 Aspirations of the World: A Chain of Opals (an eclectic Bible). Child's final message in eliminating prejudice.

1879 Tribute to Garrison in the *Atlantic* (her last article)

Over the River...
Life of Lydia Maria Child,
Abolitionist for Freedom

"I am fully aware in making this appeal to my much-afflicted and suffering brethren that I shall not only be assailed by those whose greatest earthly desires are to keep us in abject ignorance and wretchedness and who are of the firm conviction that heaven has designed us and our children to be slaves and beasts of burden to them and their children."

David Walker, 1829

Story Preface by Historians

Over the River...Life of Lydia Maria Child, Abolitionist for Freedom, is a story about one great American who just happened to have been a woman with an undying commitment to abolish what was contrary to freedom in America— the existence of slavery.

This is a woman who, for nearly 50 years, through her literary contribution was an American household name and a leading anti-slavery propagandist of the 19th century. Outside the circle of surviving abolitionists such as Harriet Beecher Stowe, Thomas Wentworth Higginson, Louisa May Alcott, Ralph Waldo Emerson, Frederick Douglass, she was only given brief public mention in obituary notices in Boston and New York newspapers, chronicling her career.

Over a century after her death, the only popular recognition of her, is the famous Thanksgiving Day poem, turned song: *Over the River and Through the Woods to Grandmother's House We Go*. It's a joyous song with verses about pleasant times in America, which is a stark contrast to what she really endured most of her life.

Over 130 years after her first anti-slavery book, *An Appeal in*

Favor of that Class of Americans Called Africans was published, the Civil Rights Movement of the 1960s used her message to forge its cause, and even today, her ideas in *An Appeal* seem to resonate loudly in a society that is still plagued with racial problems. Written in 1833, the *Appeal* called for ending all forms of racial discrimination—from lifting employment bans and integrating schools to abolishing anti-miscegenation laws. Child's *Appeal* remains relevant because it not only discusses America's social ills, but it also gives remedies by practicing tolerance and racial equality.

The great mystery of her life is: How did Lydia Maria Child survive against all odds to pursue such an unpopular cause?

The well regarded historian, Milton Meltzer, co-author of *Lydia Maria Child Selected Letters 1817-1880* remembers the attempts to obtain funding to publish Child's selected letters:

Milton Meltzer:

"A group of feminist scholars—women, had challenged the National Historical Publications Commission on the ground that they existed only to publish presidential papers, and some of those run for 10, 15, 20, or 30 volumes—quite costly, quite expensive to research, and yet they'd never done a woman and women had not yet been elected president, and no one knew when, if ever that would happen, so they thought that was an unfair use of taxpayers' money since women paid taxes, too, so the answer of the commission was, 'Well, why don't you people get together and tell us—prepare a list of women you think worthy of a grant. They did that, and since they alphabetized the list, lo and behold, Child, beginning with C, was at the head of the list, and so, promptly, the University of Massachusetts decided to apply for a grant from the same commission that pays for the presidential papers to do it, and, luckily, they got the grant, and I was, together with my women colleagues, able to do the first book under those conditions."

The leading Child historian, Carolyn Karcher, Ph.D., explains why she chose to spend more than ten years of her life to research and write *The First Woman in the Republic*:

Carolyn Karcher:

"She was somebody who was working on issues that were still so extremely relevant to us today. The issue of race has not gone away; in fact, it's become increasingly important, and what interested me in Child was that she was a white person who really believed in equality, who was willing to put her life on the line, to make sacrifices to bring racial equality about. And I felt that both white youth—white people and black people needed to be aware of this kind of role model—that often, the more one learns about American history, the more disillusioned one gets with many, many of the leading figures, like Thomas Jefferson."

Dr. Lori Kenschaft, author of the children's book, *Lydia Maria Child: The Quest for Racial Justice* categorizes Child's importance in shaping America:

Lori Kenschaft:

"I think there were three major things that she was involved in: one, obviously, the one she's best known for is abolitionism; the second was trying to have Native Americans be treated decently in their land and to have an opportunity to integrate into the mainstream of American society; and then third, and this was something that she was more ambivalent about—to have women have economic, political, social, cultural rights and, particularly, as she got later in her life. The key underlying all of these is her belief that people should be judged as individuals, not as members of groups or classes, as she put it. That, whenever you make a choice about how to treat somebody, it should be in relation to who that individual is."

Ann Flowers, a children's librarian at the Wayland Public Library in Massachusetts, remembers Lydia Maria Child's literary impact on children:

Ann Flowers:

"Oh, I am impressed because she was a woman way ahead of her time. She was, from the children's literature point of view, the only thing I think you would remember her for is the founding of the Juvenile

Miscellany, which was the first American children's magazine, and the fact that she was the editor of a newspaper in New York at a time when women didn't even have jobs and that she wrote letters to anybody—she wrote to the president, she wrote to the governor, she was friends with everybody, she was very influential, and for her, a poor woman—she never had much money, she didn't have much support from anybody—her husband didn't help her a great deal—to achieve as much as she achieved in her life, showed a character of extreme strength and beliefs that carried her forward that were so strong that you couldn't stop her."

Deborah Clifford, author of *Crusader for Freedom: A Life of Lydia Maria Child* remembers her research of Child:

Deborah Clifford:

"She said that—of women—that it is better not to talk about our rights but simply to go ahead and do what had to be done, and that's very much the way—she didn't join—she wasn't really interested in joining the women's suffrage movement, she disapproved of giving women the vote before blacks—on the other hand, she believed that women should have equal rights with men, and she just simply felt that it was something that she did best by just being herself, in a sense—promoting best by being herself."

Chapter One

Heritage

Lydia Francis was born in 1802 in Medford, Massachusetts, a town of 1,400 citizens near the Mystic River, known for its brick making and shipbuilding. Lydia was the daughter of Convers and Susannah Francis. Her father was a descendant of a British indentured servant who arrived in America in 1636, just 2 years prior to the ship named *Desire,* which anchored in Boston with the first African slaves.

By 1641, Massachusetts Bay and Plymouth were the first colonies to authorize slavery through legislation as part of the Body of Liberties. Even though slavery was a part of Medford's way of life for 200 years, beginning when a Medford sea captain returned from the West Indies with a cargo of cotton and tobacco, salt, and Africans, Medford reputedly became the first Freesoiler town to prevent a runaway slave from returning to the South against his will.

The citizens of Medford still pride themselves on being the first township prior to abolishing slavery in Massachusetts to assist

Belinda, an elderly black slave, to petition the Commonwealth of Massachusetts for reparation after her owner's death. The petition was accepted by the state and approved by John Hancock. Until her death, Belinda was paid over 15 pounds annually from the Isaac Royall estate, whose beautiful home still stands in Medford, centuries after the revolutionists overcame it.

By 1787, in the wake of the American Revolution, because of a combination of moral repulsion and economic disinterest, slavery in Massachusetts, Pennsylvania, Rhode Island, and Connecticut was abolished.

Lydia Francis was the granddaughter of Benjamin Francis, a fiery revolutionist, who boasted of how many Redcoats he shot during the American Revolution at Concord. It was said that the Francis men were sturdy and durable as the cloth they wove, but, ironically, it is one of the Francis women, Lydia, who was anointed by the great 19th century abolitionist leader, William Lloyd Garrison, as the First Woman in the Republic.

The year 1801, when Thomas Jefferson was inaugurated as the third president of the United States and just months before Lydia's birth, political and racial mudslinging in the press over slavery was already in full bloom. One cartoon titled by a federalist satirist called Jefferson "a philosophic cock." The satirist was duly referencing Jefferson's alleged liaisons with his slave, Sally Hemings, of Monticello, and a pun on the Gaelic cock, a symbol of Jefferson's beloved France.

Chapter One: Heritage

> "...The amalgamation of whites with blacks produces a degradation to which no lover of his country, no lover of excellence in the human character, can innocently consent."
>
> Thomas Jefferson, Notes on Virginia 1781

In a white supremacist stance on race mixing, Jefferson, the father of American democracy, publicly stated his position on miscegenation. His statement is a stark reminder of what many historians believe was his and America's hypocrisy about race mixing. As democracy took its form in America, the uncertainty of its future was ever present, with the slave question being at the crux of the instability.

"We hold these Truths to be self-evident, that all Men are created equal…"
"We the People of the United States…"

Lydia Maria Child would later use the very premise of freedom and inalienable rights drafted in the *Declaration of Independence* and the *Constitution of the United States of America* to argue passionately against oppression of Native Americans, blacks, and women.

CHAPTER ONE: HERITAGE

Lydia's childhood home in Medford was remembered by Lydia as an industrious place, where she along with her siblings, helped prepare the popular Medford crackers that were sold throughout New England. But the question of slavery deeply divided Lydia's family. Her father detested it. Her oldest brother James, a New England farmer known as a pro-slaver, was embarrassed by his sister's later public stand against slavery. Her favorite brother, Convers Jr., prominent Unitarian minister and Transcendentalist, although not a fervid abolitionist, later supported Lydia's views on immediate emancipation. One of Lydia's sisters, Mary Preston, and her husband, a probate judge, opposed slavery and its expansion.

As the northern opinions against slavery became more antagonistic toward the south, the south became more uncompromising to protect its rights, giving rise to sectional aggression for and against slavery.

Lydia's surviving letters recount her moral principles being fostered by her parents, although there is little known information about Lydia's relationship with her mother, who died of tuberculosis at 48-years-old and when Lydia was just 12 years old.

Carolyn Karcher:

"The one thing that we do know about Child—the one place where she talks about her mother, is she writes a story for her children's magazine, the *Juvenile Miscellany,* called "My Mother's Grave," and she tells a story of coming back home from school one day, having had a very bad day, as one can have, and instead of being able to unload her bad day on her mother and get support and sympathy, she found her mother looking paler and weaker than usual. Her mother said, according to this story, "Won't my daughter bring a glass of water for her poor, sick mother?" And so she flounced out of the room, got the glass of water, she banged it down on the night table, and she left without kissing her mother good night or saying goodbye, and then she found that she couldn't sleep, and she finally got out of bed to go speak to her mother, to apologize for her bad behavior, and learned that her mother had died in the course of the night. We don't know, of course, how true this story is in its details, but it rings emotionally true, and whether it's literally true or not, what it seems to say to me is that she wanted love and attention from her mother which she wasn't getting."

During Lydia's childhood, there were no literary influences in her family or community except for her brother, Convers Jr., who was known as an avid reader. Families who struggled financially usually dispensed with education and limited their reading to the Bible and didactic works.

Lydia wrote that she attended:

> "A common town school where Tom, Dick, and Harry, everybody's boy and everybody's girl, went as a matter of course."
>
> **Lydia Francis**

Chapter One: Heritage

In spite of all the daily rigor of work, somehow Lydia, from age 6, found ways to appreciate literature. Lydia later attended a private female academy and seminary to complete her primary education. Lydia's brother, Convers, was the first in her family to attend college. Unfortunately, Lydia was deprived of the same higher educational opportunities because colleges for women were unavailable in America until 1833, when Oberlin College was the first coeducational college to enroll female students. By then, Lydia was a well-regarded and sometimes much-hated author.

With much discouragement for Lydia's thirst for reading, after her mother's death, her father sent her to live with her sister, Mary, and her husband in Norridgewock, Maine, to learn the prescribed role of the female. Although she adapted to homemaking, by 14, Lydia was known to have sat with her brother-in-law in his parlor, listening to judges and lawyers as they discussed the influence of slavery on the politics of the United States.

Feeling abandoned by both her mother and father, young Lydia found comfort in the books she read, often remembering how she entertained her schoolmates with imaginative stories she created.

Lydia later absorbed much of her knowledge from reading Convers' books. She credited Convers with encouraging her passion for knowledge, but even Convers could not control her opinions. At 15, in her earliest surviving letter to him, she challenged him. She expressed her dislike of the author, John Milton's assertion of superiority over females in his poem *Paradise Lost*.

Lydia was raised Calvinist and was profoundly spiritual, but she was always in search of an organized religion that could deeply touch her spirit. In a letter to Convers at 18-years-old, responding to his concerns about her becoming a member of the Swedenborgian church:

> "You need not fear my becoming a Swedenborgian. I am in more danger of wrecking on the rocks of skepticism than of stranding on the shoals of fanaticism. I am apt to regard a system of religion and as I do any other beautiful theory, it plays round the imagination but fails to reach the heart. I wish I could find some religion in which my heart and understanding could unite."
>
> **Lydia Francis**

Carolyn Karcher: "She was very interested in the mystical visions of the seer, Emanuel Swedenborg, who had founded the Church of the New Jerusalem, as the Swedenborgians called themselves, and she began going to the Swedenborgian church, and she read a great deal in the mystical treatises of Swedenborg. And one way in which Swedenborgianism, I think, did appeal to her was that Swedenborg did have room for Africans in his scheme of things. However, the Swedenborgian church was very narrow-minded, and when Child became an ardent supporter of the anti-slavery movement, her minister, Thomas Worcester, made it very clear that he didn't like this and that he would not support and would not allow members of his congregation to become abolitionists and that he wanted his church in no way associated with abolitionism. So she was, basically, forced out of a church that had been, for her, a place that offered her spiritual nutriment."

Chapter One: Heritage

Still in search of a spiritual connection with organized religion, Lydia allowed her brother, Convers to baptize her in his church. She later wrote:

> "Suffice it to say that some associations of childhood make the name of Lydia unpleasant to me. I added the name Maria when I was baptized at 20-years-old. I was then in search of religion that would help my spiritual growth. They did not. They never seemed alive. I believe the name of Maria was all the benefit I derived from baptism."
>
> **Lydia Maria Child**

In 1824, Lydia's childhood religion of Calvinism was now secondary to Unitarianism in Boston, which controlled the institutions of power. Young Harriet Beecher Stowe, the future author of *Uncle Tom's Cabin*, remembered at 14-years-old her arrival with her father, the Presbyterian clergyman and abolitionist, Lyman Beecher, in Boston in 1825:

> "All the literary men of Massachusetts were Unitarians. All the trustees and professors of Harvard College were Unitarians. All the elite of wealth and fashion crowded Unitarian churches."
>
> **Young Harriet Beecher Stowe**

Even though Maria accepted the Unitarian practice, the search for a religion that could touch her soul continued; yet, her literary career was blossoming.

Chapter Two

Maria's Fictional Stories:
Hobomok, Juvenile Miscellany, Evenings in New England, The Rebels, and *The Juvenile Miscellany* Children's Magazine

Maria spent many years repressing her feelings about the changing roles of women in society. Being denied the education her brother received did trigger, early on, a drive to prove men wrong about their ancient beliefs that women were incapable of deep thought. *Hobomok* was Maria's first plea for racial and religious tolerance. It was the first American novel written about Native Americans and white settlers in the colonies, where the story embraced love and assimilation instead of a story based on wars of extermination. Ironically, it was Maria's father's financial support that enabled her to publish and distribute *Hobomok*.

Maria, realizing that writing novels was considered a male's sphere, was in fear of public censure, and she thus initially authored *Hobomok* anonymously. A few months after its release, the *North American Review* magazine found the plot in *Hobomok* to be in poor taste because of the interracial union between a Wampanoag Indian man and a white woman. This was the beginning of Maria's literary career facing harsh criticism and praise at the same time.

After the *North American Review's* negative critique, *Hobomok* left her in considerable debt to her father. With the encouragement of her new found mentor, George Ticknor, an influential figure in the Boston literary circles and a professor at Harvard, Maria re-released *Hobomok* and acknowledged herself as the writer. To Maria's surprise, one year later, the *North American Review* favored *Hobomok* and the woman author. Encouraged by the review and her notoriety, Maria continued writing with great enthusiasm.

Carolyn Karcher:

"What she saw was that, although she loved writing novels and although novels gave her a certain fame, she had the doors of Boston's literary salons opened to her, and she was lionized as the "brilliant Miss Francis." That was all very well, but she couldn't make money off her novels, so she was asked to start a children's magazine based on how popular and how effective people thought 'Evenings in New England' was. So, in September of 1826, she started what became the first children's magazine to survive. Within a few months, she already had 850 subscribers. She was able to make $300 a year on the *Miscellany*, which was enough to support her, and the *Miscellany*

Chapter Two: Maria's Fictional Stories

lasted from 1826 until 1834. Children used to sit on the doorsteps of their homes in Boston on the days that the *Miscellany* was supposed to be delivered. Each child who got it would have all of the other children reading it over her shoulder and leafing through it in their excitement. That's how popular this magazine was. What is fascinating, also, is the number of children who grew up on the *Miscellany* who then became abolitionists or women's rights activists or advocates of Native American rights. In other words, the *Miscellany* really raised children's consciousness at a very early age—got them interested in issues that they would devote their lives to fighting for."

Thomas Wentworth Higginson, a great abolitionist who attributes his involvement in the abolitionist movement to Maria, remembered her magazine this way:

> "She came before us as some kindly and omnipresent aunt, beloved forever by the heart of childhood, someone gifted with all lore and furnished with unfathomable resources, someone discoursing equal delight to all members of the household."
>
> Pastor Thomas Wentworth Higginson,
Abolitionist & Colonel
The First South Carolina Volunteers, Civil War

From her adoring readers, Maria received valuable gifts, jewels, beautiful dresses, social invitations, and admiring letters. Flattered by her popularity, Maria realized that she had made it beyond her wildest dreams. She also knew that her popularity was a means to successfully effect social change. Living the life of a popular writer, Maria was enjoying the comforts of success. At 23-years-old, she was already mingling among the guests at General Lafayette's grand reception in Boston.

Her next novel, *The Rebels, A Tale of The Revolution* dedicated to George Ticknor, was written using many of the characters of the American Revolution. The events Maria described seemed so real that many believed the sermon and the patriotic speech Maria created were actually delivered in the 1760s. Her imaginary orations were compiled in schoolbooks and recited by students.

True Love: David and Maria
In all that was wonderful in Maria's life, love was missing until she met David Lee Child, who was 8 years her senior and a known political radical. He was a lawyer and editor for the *Massachusetts Journal*, a Whig publication, and she, a schoolteacher. Living in the home of her brother, Convers, in Watertown, Massachusetts, when they met, Maria wrote in her diary:

> "On December 2, 1824, Mr. Child dined with us at Watertown. He possesses the rich fund of an intelligent traveler without the slightest twinge of a traveler's vanity."
>
> **Lydia Maria Francis**

Chapter Two: Maria's Fictional Stories

The smitten David wrote in his diary:

"The ethereal high-soul, high-reaching Maria—the elegant, pure, powerful-minded Maria. I know of no mind with which it seems to me my soul could hold such sweet converse as with the elegant, susceptible, correct and brilliant spirit which animates the pleasing, beautiful form of Maria. She is the only lady in Watertown who has made any impression upon me of a serious and enduring kind—in essence to say, of a tender kind."

David Lee Child

Needless to say, David swept Maria off her feet. A letter to her sister, Mary Preston:

> "Dear sister: Indeed, I am happy, happy beyond my own imagination, and that is saying much. Suffice it to say that on Friday, the 18th of October, 1827, I received an epistle from D. L. Child, esquire, and that on the same day an answer was returned which sealed my fate, which every hour's acquaintance with Mr. C. leads me more and more to think will be a happy one."
>
> **Lydia Maria Francis**

After a four yearlong courtship, despite her father's disapproval of David, Maria and David married. As a woman, Maria faced many constraints, but it was not until she married David that she realized the magnitude of relinquishing her economic freedom. David's legal and financial battles carried over into their marriage.

Lori Kenschaft:

"There were two big things going on: one was that her husband was very financially irresponsible—had a tendency to spend money he did not have, and then she had to make up the difference somehow or see him become just deeper and deeper in debt; and two, that the law of coverture, of a covered woman, the way they put it—the man and wife had become one and that one is the man, so he had the financial rights and legal responsibility, whereas she had the actual responsibility."

David did more for Maria's self-esteem than anyone she could imagine. He convinced young Maria that one-day their money problems would be resolved. With all that was troubling in their relationship, Maria and David maintained mutual admiration, particularly on their quest for emancipating the slave and promoting Indian rights.

Chapter Three

Slavery And Democracy: The Great Cotton Conflict

Prior to the invention of the Cotton Gin in 1793, people's interpretation of democracy in the *American Constitution* varied among the states. Among many of the New England Federalists, there was always a push to delete the three-fifths clause from the Constitution because this clause allowed the slave states to count three-fifths of their slave population as the basis for determining how many representatives they would have in Congress. It gave them a higher number of representatives than they otherwise would have had. It also increased the size of their Electoral College delegations. The three-fifths clause thus gave the slave states disproportionate power to influence both legislation and presidential elections.

Unfortunately, by 1800, the New England Federalists' sentiments about the three-fifths slave clause virtually dried up. To placate the north, the American Colonization Society, or ACS, was formed in 1816 by Virginian congressman Charles Fenton Mercer and supported by the popular southern statesman

Henry Clay. The ACS sought to ship manumitted slaves and free blacks to Africa, allegedly to provide them with a better life. Some of the captains of the ships, like Paul Cuffee, were African Americans and supported the plan, but many African Americans disapproved of the ACS program. James Forten, a leader of a prominent abolitionist and women's suffrage family in Philadelphia, attacked the colonization society's belief that blacks were aliens in America. Forten said,

> "To separate the blacks from the whites is as impossible as to bail out the Delaware with a bucket."
>
> **James Forten**

Forten's solution was to have the ACS put their energies into providing funds for black apprenticeships, which would do more to uplift the race and overcome prejudice. The African American community believed that the purported benevolent attempt by the ACS was insincere and a ploy to quash discussion that was brewing over black freedom. It was Maria's contention as well.

A Relationship Made In Heaven?

A relationship seemingly made in heaven, the pro-slavery north benefited greatly from the plantation south. Cotton was King. It had become the most valuable staple commodity in the Atlantic world. It stimulated the economy and the spread of slavery. The south, being encouraged by leaders such as Henry Clay and John C. Calhoun, viewed slavery as a free market economy. They asserted that as long as the north sustained a laissez-faire policy of non-interference, that the south would remain in the Union and continue feeding the northern economy.

Chapter Three: Slavery and Democracy

Between 1815 and 1820, cotton production doubled in the south. Profits from slavery soared as cotton production expanded from Georgia and South Carolina to Louisiana, Mississippi, and Alabama. In the upper south and Deep South, slaves were becoming more expensive to purchase. The south, feeling constrained by the inability to import more Africans because of the 1808 congressional ban on the transatlantic slave trade, resorted to accepting Africans illegally brought from Africa. Slave owners also forced their male slaves to breed with childbearing slave women on the plantation. Many slave owners raped the slave women to increase their slave population, although the slave owners did not consider it rape since the women were their property. As America acquired more land and admitted more states into the Union, particularly Florida, Maine, then Arkansas, Illinois, and Missouri that were a part of the Louisiana Purchase, the number of slave states and non-slave states was equal.

Prior to its statehood, Missourians believing that they would be admitted into the Union as a slave state were rudely awakened by northern so-called Republican Restrictionists, particularly Congressman James Tallmadge, who, in 1819, introduced two amendments to the resolution to admit Missouri as a state but only if it banned slavery and released all slaves of the age of 25 born in the state after its admission. Missourians, feeling attacked, threatened disunion before they were approved to enter as a state.

The south feeling pressured, slipped further into a distrusting relationship with the north. The south realized that there would be a legislative battle at every turn. To placate both sides, compromises and deal-making in Congress and the executive branch ensued. The biggest compromise was the Missouri Controversy, or Compromise of 1820, that included a redrafting of the Missouri state constitution that would not bar free blacks or bi-racials from entering the state if Missouri wanted statehood. The compromise triggered internal conflicts in Missouri between anti-slavers and pro-slavers. To placate the north, Maine was admitted as a free state and Missouri as a slave state, and slavery was banned from all remaining territories within the Louisiana Purchase north of latitude 36 degree 30 north parallel. The Compromise, not really satisfying to anyone, was said to have deepened further the sentiment for disunion.

To promote the Union, Henry Clay and John C. Calhoun leading the south, while John Quincy Adams and John Tyler and others leading the north, focused on shaping the economy. Meanwhile, by 1826, a group of black Bostonian businessmen like John Moore, founded the Massachusetts General Colored Association to fight for an end to slavery and the ACS movement. It became Boston's primary abolitionist organization. The ACS, determined to move African Americans out of the country to dampen the fears of insurrections, encouraged by manumitted slaves and free blacks, infiltrated the temperance, Bible, and Sunday school movements of the north and south to seek public and government support.

Maria's Domestic Advice Book and David's Debts: *The Frugal Housewife, The Mother's Book,* and *The Little Girl's Own Book*

Continuing her emphasis on shaping women, Maria, in 1829, published the very first American domestic advice book for the lower middle class titled *The Frugal Housewife*. Drawing from personal experience, she shared her own recipes and homeopathic remedies. Her early role as a homemaker to her sister's children allowed Maria to give cogent advice on parenting and housekeeping. After selling thousands of copies, *The Frugal Housewife* reached its 33rd edition by 1855.

> "My advice is to look frequently to the pails to see that nothing is thrown to the pigs which should have been in the grease pot. Look to the grease pot and see that nothing is there which might have served to nourish your own family or a poor one."
>
> **Lydia Maria Child**

Every dollar Maria earned continued to pay off David's debts. Though embarrassed, but not too proud to ask, she borrowed money from wealthy friends and requested advances on her work. She sold the furniture she'd purchased after their nuptials. In spite of their financial problems, her domestic advice books, *The Mother's Book*, and *The Little Girl's Own Book*, continued to sell well.

The Beginning of the End to Slavery: Black Civil Rights and Women's Rights Brewing

In 1829, David Walker, an influential black figure in the African American community of Boston's Beacon Hill, wrote his treatise, *An Appeal to the Colored Citizens of the World*. In a minister-like delivery to the all black congregation, David Walker substantially referenced two important 18th century documents, the

Declaration of Independence and the U.S. Constitution, to argue his points against slavery and the ACS:

> "Now we have to determine whose advice we will take respecting this all-important matter— whether we will adhere to Mr. Clay and his slave holding party, who have always been our oppressors and murderers and who are colonizing us more through apprehension than humanity.... I am awfully afraid that pride, prejudice, avarice, and blood will before long prove the final ruin of this happy republic or land of liberty. Can anything be a greater mockery of religion than the way in which it is conducted by the Americans? They chain and handcuff us and our children and drive us around the country like brutes and go into the house of the God of justice to return Him thanks for having aided them in their infernal cruelties inflicted upon us.... Will the Lord not stop them, preachers and all? Oh, Americans, Americans, I call God— call angels—I call men to witness that your destruction is at hand and will be speedily consummated unless you repent."
>
> **David Walker, 1829**

David Walker's *Appeal* attacked President Jefferson's contention that the black race occupied the lowest human position and was barely distinguishable from animals. Countering Jefferson's belief, Walker asserted that blacks had humanity and that white Americans were at fault for creating their degraded existence. After the *Appeal* went through three editions, David Walker was found dead under mysterious circumstances but not before

Chapter Three: Slavery and Democracy

he made a deep social impression.

In 1829, William Lloyd Garrison, a fiery, young pressman who once admired Henry Clay and supported the ACS's concept, began to question both. By 1831, under the influence of African Americans, he did an about-face, criticizing the ACS as a slaveholder's plot. During a time when very few Americans cared about the slavery question, unknown to each other, young William Lloyd Garrison and Lydia Maria Child believed that religion had the moral answers to change opinions. However, Garrison's approach to obtaining social change was brash, while Maria's was subtle. Garrison, witnessing the influence the ACS had on the churches, decided to use similar tactics of moral persuasion to change attitudes. His first order of business was to end slavery in the District of Columbia because Congress had direct jurisdiction there; next, immediately abolish slavery, not send blacks to Africa or anywhere else; and then educate the free black population and elevate them to a rank with the whites. As a lone white writer dissenting against the ACS migration efforts, William Lloyd Garrison published, in 1832, his first and only book, *Thoughts on African Colonization* or *An Impartial Exhibition of the Doctrines, Principles, and Purposes of the American Colonization Society, Together with the Resolutions, Addresses, and Remonstrances of the Free People of Color*:

> "This is the question and the only question: whether it is not the sacred duty of the nation to abolish the system of slavery now and to recognize the people of color as brethren and countrymen who have been unjustly treated and covered with unmerited shame."
>
> **William Lloyd Garrison**

Meanwhile, in his *Liberator* newspaper, young Garrison publicly condemned Walker's plea for insurrection:

> "I deny the right of any people to fight for liberty and so far am a Quaker in principle. I do not justify the slaves in their rebellion; yet, I do not condemn them and applaud similar conduct in white men."
>
> **William Lloyd Garrison**

But Garrison understood that the underlying cause for these malevolent outbursts was the institution of slavery, an institution in which blacks lived, feared, and reacted out of self- preservation. Despite his pacifist beliefs, Garrison's newspaper, *The Liberator*, was to southerners an incendiary device encouraging insurrection. Even though Garrison deplored violence, he sympathized with the oppressed in spite of the violence. This was the beginning of a moral quandary in which Garrison had to decide if the means justified the end. Maria Child faced the same decision.

Insurrection In Virginia

During the hot summer days of August, 1831, in Southampton County, Virginia, a contingent of slaves, led by the visionary slave preacher, Nat Turner, rose up against their masters, insurrected, and brutally killed 55 white people, including children, before being caught by the state militia. In retaliation, soldiers and vigilantes terrorized slave quarters across the county, brutally killing over 100 slaves and savagely mutilating hundreds more.

Carolyn Karcher:

"David had strongly defended Nat Turner in his newspaper, the *Massachusetts Journal,* which was still running at that time. Maria and David had had kind of a running debate over Nat Turner and over the defense of violence. Basically, Child's position was very much like Garrison's position, where they both considered themselves pacifists, but they both felt that it was not the right of white people to tell black people that they couldn't win their freedom in any way that they could."

Echoing Walker's and Garrison's words, Maria Child dismissed the stereotypes of blacks as a shallow pretext for depriving blacks of all the rights of men. Walker's message touched Maria. Through the *Juvenile Miscellany* magazine, she expressed publicly her views that blacks, like the Indians, could assimilate into the American society through intermarriage.

"It has been said that a stone thrown into the sea agitates more or less every drop in that vast expanse of waters. So it may be with the influence we exert on the minds and hearts of the young. It may spread a salutary and sacred influence over the whole life and through the whole mass of the character of the child. It may go down from one generation to another, widening and deepening its influence as it goes, reaching forth with various modifications, more or less direct, 'til the track of its agency shall be completely beyond human calculation."

Lydia Maria Child

Chapter Three: Slavery and Democracy

The *Juvenile Miscellany* featured many stories about people of color. Her stories intentionally targeted white mothers to help them develop sensitivity toward cultures unlike their own. Maria had thrown the metaphorical stone of tolerance into the sea of human consciousness to agitate and invoke moral response.

Carolyn Karcher:

"What David did was get her into political editing, which she had never done before. He made her the literary editor of the *Massachusetts Journal,* and a lot of her early writings were published in the *Massachusetts Journal,* and, in fact, her first article on interracial marriage, which gets incorporated almost in toto into An Appeal, was published anonymously in the *Massachusetts Journal.* When they got married in 1828, David was very much involved in the campaign to re-elect John Quincy Adams and to defeat Andrew Jackson. He was also very much involved in the campaign to save the Cherokee from being uprooted from their ancestral land in Georgia and forcibly moved to what's now Oklahoma. Maria was editing the literary page of the *Massachusetts Journal* and pitching in on the main editorial page, and she also wrote a very radical book at the time, which she ended up not publishing, called *The First Settlers of New England.*"

In a passage in the book, Maria envisioned what America could gain from an Indian policy of assimilation, rather than the barbaric approach of extermination.

> "By intermixing, the descendants of the Puritans might have saved the nation from the hordes of vagrants, who have been allured to our shores like vultures by the scent of prey, that they might seize on the spoils of the natives whom we have destroyed."
>
> Lydia Maria Child

Those vagrants, in Maria's view, were the penniless and unruly immigrants who thronged to Andrew Jackson's democratic party. Maria believed that Jackson's answer was to expand the process of electoral democratization, using the new class of unskilled immigrants to advance the expansion of slavery into the territories where Indians had trustingly negotiated treaties. Although Maria had not yet found her voice as a propagandist in the *First Settlers*, she had stepped into reform work and never looked back.

Abolitionism, Unionism, State Rights, and Jacksonian Politics

In the early 1830s, while the seemingly marginal group of radical abolitionists made what appeared to be little headway with their cause, labor unionism and its influence in politics was establishing its roots with democratic zeal, a move that the southern planters and businessmen scoffed at. David Child and Jackson's political opponents believed President Andrew Jackson, the icon of the new democracy, surrounded himself with corruption.

A self-proclaimed champion of the common man, Jackson's

vision of democracy excluded any role for Indians, who he believed should be pushed west of the Mississippi River and African Americans, who should remain as slaves or be freed and sent abroad. Jackson's presidential focus was to improve the economy and not succumb to anti-slavery appeals or southern radical interests. Jackson's second term brought him closer to the labor movement but increased hostilities towards southern states' rights radicals, opponents of the Indian removal program, and anti-slavery radicals.

Maria's Anguish over David /
Garrison Hails Maria "The First Woman In The Republic"
As the sole breadwinner, Maria kept herself and David afloat, paying off his debts and pursuing her writing career, which meant selling her stories to publishers for annual gift books, magazines, and newspapers. In a letter to her sister-in-law, Lydia Child:

> "I find myself looking more carefully to personal economy than I did before I was married. I certainly have denied myself every superfluity. I have dropped all my acquaintance. I never visit nor receive visits. We never ride; never go to the theater, or any place of public amusement. It seems queer to me. I used to go out so much, but after all, I am happier than I ever was."
>
> **Lydia Maria Child**

After borrowing money to keep the *Massachusetts Journal* afloat, David's political newspaper was failing, and his expenses from libel suits mounted. David lost a libel appeal. Unable to pay his debt, David spent six months in prison. While he was in prison, Maria managed the newspaper. Maria moved out of the woman's sphere, becoming the only other female editor of a newspaper, save for the famous Scottish-born liberal Frances Wright, who was the co-editor of *The Free Inquirer,* and the first woman to speak to a mixed audience of men and women. While David was serving time in jail, Maria, struggling to make ends meet, moved in with a friend and juggled editing the newspaper while continuing to write for an income.

In all of her despair, Maria wanted children but realized that, economically, it would be impossible to raise children under the many financial and social constraints they faced. Maria, staying focused as the editor of the *Massachusetts Journal,* turned David's political mudslinging newspaper into a family paper that published reviews, critiques, articles, and stories, including her own stories. Maria also gave public instruction on topics titled *Philosophy* and *Consistency, Hints to People of Moderate Fortune, Politeness,* and the most publicly recognized, *The Comparative Strength of Male and Female Intellect.* By 1832, even with Maria's attempts to revive it, the *Massachusetts Journal* folded. Maria's *Hints* and the *Comparative Strength* earlier attracted 24-year-old William Lloyd Garrison.

Garrison, impressed with Maria's articles in the *Massachusetts Journal,* gave tributes to her in the prominent anti-slavery newspaper out of Baltimore, Maryland, *The Genius of Universal Emancipation.* Garrison, a progressive thinker himself on women's self-determination, reprinted Maria's article, which, ironically, did not assert a doctrine of sexual equality that Frances Wright was advocating. Maria, in her eloquent and didactic style, publicly acknowledged male superiority but asserted that women had a virtuous role that could shape men to do good deeds. Wright, in taking offense to accepting male dominance over women, made a progressive statement that:

> "No woman can forfeit her individual rights of independent existence and no man assert over her any rights or power whatsoever beyond what he may exercise over her free and voluntary affections."
>
> **Frances Wright**

At least Wright, a lone star, was willing to assert her convictions amidst editorial ridicule and criticism, even from Maria Child. Garrison could not say enough about Maria's brilliant mind, comparing her work to Benjamin Franklin's *Poor Richard's Almanac*. Garrison exclaimed that:

> "There is no one equal to Mrs. Child, male or female, that comes close to her wisdom and wonderful knowledge of human nature."
>
> **William Lloyd Garrison**

After an extensive article of praise and admiration, he proclaimed Maria the "First Woman in the Republic." Garrison expressed his desire to meet the ennobling Mrs. Child. His intermediary was David Child. Garrison's first job had been as a journeyman working for David's newspaper, the *Massachusetts Journal*.

Carolyn Karcher:

"Garrison already admired her tremendously, and when he was embarked on his crusade against slavery, he looked around for the best literary talent that he could find to help him win the hearts and minds of the American people for emancipation, and Child was the first person he thought of, and the other great literary figure he thought of was John Greenleaf Whittier."

Garrison met Maria just at the threshold of organizing his anti-slavery newspaper, *The Liberator*, and recruiting members for the newly founded New England Anti-Slavery Society. David was one of the founding members of drafting the organization's constitution.

In 1830, Maria wrote her first anti-slavery story in the *Juvenile Miscellany—The St. Domingo Orphans*, then another story *Jumbo and Zairee*. In *The St. Domingo Orphans*, Maria suggested that the continuation of slavery would be a greater threat than immediate abolition.

Garrisonians

Garrison's book, *Thoughts on African Colonization*, struck a chord throughout the black and white abolitionist circles and gained recruits to the cause. His message even appealed to some of the moderate reformers in the ACS, particularly his friend, Reverend Samuel May, who echoed Jefferson's sentiment that abolishing slavery could only be accomplished through political and physical separation of the races. Garrison, knowing the major challenge he was up against, told his friend May that if his efforts to abolish slavery failed, at least he would have a hand in raising the political stature of the free black population through his newspaper. *The Liberator* reached well beyond his 500 subscribers in the inaugural issue. The content included equal treatment of blacks, self-advancement through education, and employment skills, united political action, and a mass rejection of the colonization efforts. Week after week, Garrison published the *Liberator*, gaining more subscribers and enemies as well. Even his friend, Samuel May, asked him to moderate his indignation and cool down his rhetoric.

May was remembered saying, "You are all on fire."

Garrison replied, "When the poor, downtrodden slaves tell me that I am too harsh, then I will soften my language. Brother May, I have need to be all on fire, for I have mountains of ice about me to melt." Garrison's life was threatened. He was told that men would take his life and no one would be the wiser.

> "I hold my life at a cheap rate. If the assassin takes it away, the Lord will raise up another and better advocate in my stead."
>
> **William Lloyd Garrison**

The south began an organized campaign to suppress Garrison's *Liberator* and Garrison himself. The District of Columbia passed a law prohibiting free blacks from taking copies of the *Liberator* out of the post office. The penalties were a fine of $20 and 30 days in jail. Further in the south, grand juries indicted Garrison in absentia for distributing incendiary matter. Soon, a bounty of $5,000 to bring him to the south to be tried for seditious libel was available for kidnappers to consider. Pro-slavery politicians challenged the north's commitment to keeping a happy union, using Garrison as their bait. Southern laws against slaves tightened, taking a hold of Maria's conscience.

Maria's Literary Bombshell and the Personal Attacks Against Her

In 1833, while researching and writing biographies of women at the prestigious private library, the Boston Athenaeum, where only one other woman, Hannah Adams, had the honor of free privileges, the lionized Maria published her first anti-slavery book, *An Appeal in Favor of that Class of Americans Called Africans*. This was the year the *North American Review* acclaimed her as the "Foremost Woman Writer in America." Drawing from international authors and works published in the *Liberator*, Maria called for immediate emancipation without compensation to the slave owners. She argued against colonization in Africa, defended racial equality, and indicted racism in the south and the north. During this time, women were at first, not allowed to join the New England Anti-Slavery Society. Their influence in pamphleteering and petitioning to abolish the slave trade and slavery in the District of Columbia were bold steps out of woman's sphere.

In 1833, as members of the Boston Female Anti-Slavery Society, one of the first organizations of its kind, Maria, along with other women reformers, black and white, worked to push for the immediate emancipation of the slaves. Even with the financial constraints, Maria, along with her friend, Louisa Loring, sponsored the first successful anti-slavery fair in 1834 to raise money for the cause.

CHAPTER THREE: SLAVERY AND DEMOCRACY

In retaliation for her involvement in the reform movement and writing *An Appeal*, northern pro-slavers rejected her. One politician was seen dropping her book to the ground with a pair of tongs. People burned her books as well as anti-slavery material. The conflict was heating up, and Maria was in the center being attacked. Like a bad dream, Maria was caught in a whirlwind. Her favorite brother, Convers, cautioned her not to speak poorly of the southerners. Her brother, James, a pro-slaver and Jacksonian Democrat, turned hostile toward Maria, stating that he could not stomach either niggers or nigger-lovers. Her father, though a sympathizer with the cause, blamed David for the financial hardships the couple suffered as a result of their anti- slavery activism. Maria's rich friends were cold toward her, literary contemporaries became distant, and the final blow—her patron, George Ticknor, blacklisted her and vowed to ostracize anyone who violated a ban against her. The Boston Athenaeum withdrew her free library privileges that George Ticknor was instrumental in getting for his prized author. *The Mother's Book* immediately went out of print, and *The Frugal Housewife* sales dropped. Maria's income diminished to almost nothing. At the same time, *An Appeal* catapulted her to the forefront of the abolitionist movement alongside Garrison. *An Appeal* had moved Maria into political influence that was unmatched by any woman.

No longer bound by gender or class, Maria was now a priceless political propagandist on behalf of the oppressed in the United States. Abolitionist press reviewers hailed *An Appeal* as a powerful support to the anti-slavery cause. *An Appeal's* influence was not confined just to woman. Maria's calm and rational tone in

35

the book allowed facts to speak for themselves. Her style of framing conclusions as rhetorical questions that produced palpable reaction in the reader succeeded in converting people who were turned off to the fiery style of Garrison.

The prominent Boston Unitarian minister, William Ellery Channing, who dissuaded his parishioners from joining anti-slavery societies, read the *Appeal* and became a notable recruit and mediator between abolitionists and conservative northern religious opponents.

Maria had touched the depths of moral consciousness of legislators, publishers, ministers, writers, the average citizen—even some Transcendentalists, like the poet, James Russell Lowell, who later gave homage to her in a long poem, using the title of her Transcendental book, *Philothea*, to describe her impact on the people:

> "There comes Philothea, her face all aglow. She has just been dividing some poor creature's woe.... The pole science tells us the magnet controls, but she is a magnet to emigrant poles and folks with a mission that nobody knows, throng thickly about her as bees 'round a rose..."
> **James Russell Lowell**

Abolitionism clearly came between Convers Jr. and Maria, but they continued to share their love of Transcendentalism. Maria dedicated *Philothea* to Convers.

Carolyn Karcher:

"A lot of people who were attracted to Transcendentalism were, in fact also attracted to abolitionism—Ellis

Loring, for instance. But in the early days, Emerson himself was not, and the problem with Transcendentalism for her in the beginning was that it was too Transcendental. In other words, it was mystical and visionary and philosophical but really not grounded in fighting for a just society."

As a role model for women, Maria successfully displayed the intellectual fortitude of which women were capable but believed they did not have.

Deborah Clifford:

"She said that—of women—that it is better not to talk about our rights but simply to go ahead and do what had to be done, and that's very much the way—she didn't join—she wasn't really interested in joining the women's suffrage movement, she disapproved of giving women the vote before blacks—on the other hand, she believed that women should have equal rights with men, and she just simply felt that it was something that she did best by just being herself, in a sense— promoting best by being herself."

Maria Blames Herself for David's Impractical Business Schemes/ 1835 "The Year of the Mob"

Unfortunately, Maria's public strength did not carry over into her private life. She believed that it was her unwomanly ambitions that drove David to make poor decisions, competing with her.

To David, she wrote:

> "I wish I had been as uniformly good and kind as you have been, but my ambitious and impatient temperament needed a world of trouble to tame it. The truth is, I have formed the habit of depending on you for all my sunshine."
>
> Lydia Maria Child

Exhausted, Maria continued to support David's altruistic but impractical business schemes, which caused them to lose almost everything they had including their beloved home near the harbor, which they called Cottage Place. Maria's worst fear was now realized. They were cast adrift. But the Childs were not alone in their struggles. Abolitionists supported each other within their network, but outside of it, they, too, faced public sanctions.

Hostilities peaked in 1835, considered the "Year of the Mob," continuing throughout the decade, crowds of thugs led by prominent men stormed abolitionist meetings, pelting the speakers with hard objects and rotten eggs. Lynching, vandalism in abolitionists' offices and printing presses, and arson that leveled halls, homes, and entire African American neighborhoods were a daily threat. Yet, Maria continued to publish anti-slavery material.

Helping his fellow reformers regroup from their financial mishaps, Garrison made arrangements for the Childs to sail to England with the infamous incendiary British speaker and abolitionist, George Thompson, who was instrumental in abolishing slavery in the British West Indies. They were to work as agents in

Chapter Three: Slavery and Democracy

the British anti-slavery societies, but, as luck would have it, the day they were to embark, David was sued by his former partner and served with an injunction to prevent him from leaving. Maria was devastated but believed that David would resolve matters and they'd soon make the journey to England. It never happened—at least not for Maria.

Maria was still at a crossroad in her life. Should she keep repressing her feeling about woman's prescribed role in America or aid in redefining the role of woman after seeing the frustrations women were having in the abolitionist movement? The first of its kind in 1835, a two-volume book, *The History of the Condition of Women*, explored the similarities and differences among the women of the world. She addressed very deep and important issues about women and their destinies as well as raised the prospects of change for women over time as the need for economic development increased and social roles shifted. Maria boldly compared male dominance to the system of slavery from a world historical and cross-cultural point of view. Similar to *An Appeal*, Maria eloquently made implicit and explicit comparisons between women and slaves; for example, the pricing of wives according to their beauty, like the quadroon slaves, on the auction block of New Orleans or the raffling of imported European wives to British colonists in India, Maria gave one example after another of the pervasive use of the dowry system defining marriage as an economic transaction in which wives are purchased and daughters are sold, reinforcing the widespread ancient views that wives were slaves, commodities, and inferior creatures.

Meanwhile, the slave-owning states, believing that true democracy rested on the freedom to own slaves, continued trying to suppress public discussion on the slavery question. By 1836, the south enforced the Gag Rule in Congress, which provided that all petitions, memorials, resolutions, propositions, or papers relating in any way or to any extent whatever, to the subject of slavery or the abolition of slavery shall, without being printed or referred, be laid upon the table and that no further action whatever be taken thereon. The south was furthering the north's frustration about emancipation. The northern abolitionists moved quickly to agitate communities throughout the north.

One such activist was Elijah Lovejoy, a Presbyterian minister, who owned a newspaper in Alton, Illinois. He devoted most of his newspaper, the *Alton Observer*, to anti-slavery articles. After mobs destroyed his press three times, Lovejoy, for the last time defending himself, was shot in the chest and killed. He was the first white anti-slavery leader to be killed for the cause. His murder shocked and emboldened the growing movement. Sympathy for the abolitionists increased throughout the north, fostering anti-southern sentiments, and memberships in anti-slavery societies increased.

Maria's loyalty to the cause of freedom was unrelenting, even risking her life at the hands of an angry mob. Her direct connection to a hostile world was probably with her brother, Convers. During this transitional time, Maria corresponded with him. In one letter, Convers tried to blame the mob activity on democracy, believing it was the mother of evil. Maria's reply:

Chapter Three: Slavery and Democracy

> "What is the root of the difficulty on this great question of abolition? It is not with the farmers, it is not with the mechanics—the majority of their voices would be on the right side if the question was fairly brought before them. Manufacturers who supply the south, merchants who trade with the south, politicians who trade with the south, ministers settled at the south, and editors patronized by the south are the ones who really promote mobs. Withdraw the aristocratic influence, and I should be perfectly easy to trust the cause to the good feeling of the people."
>
> Lydia Maria Child

Maria continued immersing herself in writing and editing anti-slavery stories, attending anti-slavery meetings, and maintaining long-lasting relationships with fellow abolitionists who took Maria and David in as boarders. Some of Maria's closest friends were Quakers.

Carolyn Karcher:

"She was very attracted to Quakerism and to the Quakers because of their commitment to fighting against slavery, but the Quakers were, in a sense, much akin to Puritans in wanting to eliminate everything from the religion—music, color, ritual, all of the things associated with Catholicism and Episcopalianism. But for Child, music and the visual arts were a part of her spirituality."

While on a visit to Philadelphia in 1836, Maria met two impressive Quaker women: the minister Lucretia Mott, the future pioneer for women's rights, and Angelina Grimke, a daughter of a South Carolina aristocratic slave-holding family who, with her sister Sarah, left the south to report on the horrors of the institution of slavery. Angelina's message was powerful, recruiting many non-believers to the abolitionist cause. In 1836, Angelina Grimke published *An Appeal to the Christian Women of the Southern States*, the only publication ever written by a southern white woman, imploring emancipation of the slaves.

Maria's correspondence with her brother, Convers, continued. Replying to an anxious letter on slavery from Convers, she wrote:

> "You ask me to be prudent, and I will be so, as far as is consistent with a sense of duty. A principle of despotism was admitted in the very formation of our government to sanction which our conscience have been continually silenced and sealed. In our social institutions, aristocracy has largely mingled. I believe the world will be brought into a state of order through manifold revolutions. I have examined the history of the slave too thoroughly and felt his wrongs too deeply to be prudent in the worldly sense of the term. I know too well the cruel and wicked mockery contained in all the excuses and palliations of the system."
>
> **Lydia Maria Child**

Chapter Three: Slavery and Democracy

With all the passion Maria possessed for anti-slavery work, she reportedly never stood before an audience and lectured. Just after the letter to Convers, Maria published a series of anti-slavery articles and books [*Anti-slavery Catechism, Cure of Slavery, The Fountain, The Oasis*]. At a racially integrated American anti-slavery convention in 1837, Maria was instrumental in drafting *An Appeal to the Women of the Nominally Free States*.

Maria Supports David's Beet Farming Project

In the midst of her activism, David decided to leave for England to study beet sugar production. After his return in 1838, the Childs moved to Northampton, Massachusetts, to become beet farmers. This was David's next pet project and his personal crusade on behalf of the oppressed people. From the beginning, the project was plagued with problems. Promised financial support fell through, leaving Maria with paying for farming equipment. The leased land David had planned to cultivate was rocky and full of weeds. Maria weeded for hours and days at a time. Feeling isolated among the aristocrats of Northampton, Maria secretly began missing the rewards of being a popular writer. Those who knew her as the author of the *Juvenile Miscellany* and *The Frugal Housewife* approved of her living in the town, as long as she did not agitate for black freedom. Writing to an abolitionist friend, Abby Kelley:

> "Never in my life have I witnessed so much of the lofty slave-holding spirit. Will moral influence ever reach these haughty sinners? Never! Much as I deprecate it, I am convinced that emancipation must come through violence."
>
> **Lydia Maria Child**

Even though there was disagreement over blacks and women's participation within the mainstream abolitionist movement, living in Northampton, Massachusetts, Maria experienced the cold unwillingness to help wipe out racism in America. Maria was not alone in this view. Garrison finally came to that conclusion, too, after experiencing mob violence.

> "I have ceased to believe that public opinion will ever be sincerely reformed on the question 'til long after emancipation has taken place. For generations to come, there will be a very large minority hostile to the claims of colored people."
>
> **Lydia Maria Child**

Carolyn Karcher:

"Because of the splits in the anti-slavery movement over the issues of women's rights, religion, and whether or not the movement should try to start a political party of its own or should stick with moral suasion as its main focus, what happened was that the Garrisonians and the evangelical groups split off into two different anti-slavery societies, and the evangelicals walked off with the *Emancipator*, which had been the organ of the anti-slavery movement. So they decided that what they needed was a really distinguished editor who would be able to transcend the differences between the two factions and get the anti-slavery movement refocused on its main aim, which was fighting slavery. And they asked David and Maria Child to edit the paper. And David couldn't, or didn't want to, because he was busy trying to make beet sugar succeed in Northampton, and Child agreed to do it, although this meant moving from Northampton to New York. So, from the very beginning, what she tried to do was reorient the standard toward attacking slavery rather than attacking deviations from the correct line and attacking fellow abolitionists who happened to have different opinions. She also wanted—she felt that it was crucial for the anti-slavery movement to do more outreach—to reach people who had no interest in slavery, no commitment to slavery, so she tried to make the *Standard* a family newspaper, with something in it for everybody—something that women would read, something that children would read, something that farmers would read, something that intellectuals would read, a literary component, and it worked very well."

The masthead on the 1840s newspaper reflected Maria's new statement of female empowerment, yet in the mainstream press, David and Maria were ridiculed for Maria's leadership of the

Standard. The *New York Courier* and the *Inquirer*, an anti-abolitionist Whig newspaper, scoffed:

> "The male child has not grown into puberty enough to be worthy of being promoted to at least a joint labor with his wife."
>
> **Critic, Anti-abolitionist Whig Newspaper**

Ignoring the jibes, both worked well together, with David providing mainly political editorials while Maria covered a range of anti-slavery topics. Garrison showed his support by reprinting her editorials in his newspaper, *The Liberator*. Wendell Phillips, a staunch Garrisonian, encouraged Maria to continue her style of propaganda that, he said, had:

> "Touched the ultra, the moderates, the half-converted, the fanatics, the indifferent, and the active."
>
> **Wendell Phillips**

Maria's Transcendental Loves

While living in New York, Maria became a boarder to the prominent Quaker couple, Hannah and Isaac Hopper, known for their tough and rebellious stands on slavery and for prison reform. Isaac Hopper was also known by a smaller circle of abolitionists to be a long-time protector of runaway slaves. Moving to New York, Maria almost immediately shifted her affection away from David toward several men: Ellis Loring, married to Louisa Loring, whom she loved and trusted; John Hopper, an attorney and son of the Hoppers; and the Norwegian violinist, Ole Bull, whose music...

> "...stirred the depths of my soul and kindled my whole being."
>
> Lydia Maria Child

After a full day's work, Maria found comfort in John, 13 years her junior. Her platonic relationship over time with all three men made her feel wanted, although her friend, Ellis Loring, cautioned her that courting John's feelings would lead to emotional peril. To him, she replied:

> "My charms were never very formidable and to this period, I think can hardly endanger a young man of 26, passionately fond of the beautiful. If there is danger in being absolutely necessary to each other's happiness, for the time being, we are both in great peril."
>
> Lydia Maria Child

Maria never considered herself beautiful. Later, in 1843, probably triggered by John's interest in beautiful women and the transcendental philosophy of beauty, she wrote an essay on *What is Beauty?* Her dear friend, Margaret Fuller, published it in the Transcendentalist newspaper, *The Dial*. As the months progressed, she wrote to the Lorings:

> "My affections have got so entwined around him that it would almost kill me to have to leave him. David and he and I can live together and bless each other."
>
> Lydia Maria Child

Maria exploited John's age difference in attempting to justify their closeness by calling him her adopted son. The perceived maternal role allowed her to express her feelings about him outside the conventional male/female dynamic. Sustaining a two-year courtship with John proved that her so-called motherly spirit was instead a deep love connection that Maria could not easily give up. She wrote to her friends, the Lorings:

> "His thousand little delicate attentions remind me so much of Mr. Child and, yet, are so insufficient for the cravings of a heart so fond of domestic life as mine."
> **Lydia Maria Child**

Maria realized that John was not the marrying kind, at least not in her fantasy. Maria's love was so profound that she could not hold back from writing about John, even to David:

> "How do you think I spent the 5th of July? In the most romantic way imaginable. John wanted to get me away from the noise and heat of the city. While John slept under the trees, I wrote an editorial, and, on awakening, he read aloud to me and I wove oak garlands."
> **Lydia Maria Child**

No letters survived of David's response. To her dear friends, Frances Shaw and Maria White Lowell, she described her unquenchable crush on John by expressing her feelings as:

Chapter Three: Slavery and Democracy

> "... fierce spiritual conflicts, dark wanderings, withered hopes, and uncontrollable sadness at the sight of young lovers."
>
> **Lydia Maria Child**

In researching the articles she wrote for the anti-slavery *Standard*, John accompanied Maria everywhere—even to New York's Catholic cathedrals, Jewish temples, and Swedenborgian services. He visited prisons and slums with her and absorbed the cultural life as well—the art galleries, theaters, the opera and concert halls. John's attentiveness captured Maria's heart. Her close friends sensed the breakdown in her marriage.

> "I have spent 14 years pumping water into a sieve. I must put a stop to it or die! I can put a stop to it, and I will put a stop to it!"
>
> **Lydia Maria Child**

Under a New York equity law, a wife could keep her property from her husband's creditors by transferring it to another male custodian. Maria named her trusted and dear friend, Ellis Loring, as her legal surrogate. She did not divorce David but simply gave up hope.

Maria Creates a New Style of Writing called Essays or Sketches

Living in New York, Maria created some of her best writing. She wrote volumes of children's stories and published compassionate stories in the abolitionist *Annual*. But instead of using fiction as she had in the past to analyze political issues, she created a new literary style to promote change in racial, sexual, and class attitudes through *Letters from New York*. *Letters from New York* were essays or sketches, published as a weekly column in the *National Anti-Slavery Standard* which describe the cultural diversity and the struggles of people from various walks of life in New York, still keeping with her style of being captivating, frank, personal, and conversational. In 1844, fed up with the infighting at the *National Anti-Slavery Standard*, after two years, Maria resigned as editor and discontinued her involvement in the divisive anti-slavery organizations. David became the lead editor but also resigned a year later, returning to his beet farm in Northampton.

Living very comfortably in New York, Maria enjoyed rekindling relationships with friends like Margaret Fuller, James Russell Lowell and his wife, Maria White Lowell, and acquired new acquaintances like Edgar Allen Poe. Maria enjoyed the time away from David, who traveled about working odd jobs. She continued her writing career and also published *Letters from New York* into a book series dedicated to John Hopper. Maria felt alive for the first time in a very long time.

Nothing is left in history to explain the abrupt marriage of John Hopper in 1847, but it devastated Maria, almost killing her. She moved out of the Hoppers' home and into the home of her

Quaker friends in New Rochelle, Margaret and Joseph Carpenter, to find solace. Believing she was going to die from a broken heart, Maria decided to burn 339 letters. Once she recovered, she made peace with John's decision and returned to living with the Hoppers in New York City. After deep reflection, David returned from Tennessee after working on the railroad, and the two reunited permanently, enjoying their second honeymoon. In the meantime, slave oppression worsened, and Congress grappled with the friction.

Juvenile Miscellany (Wayland Historical Society)

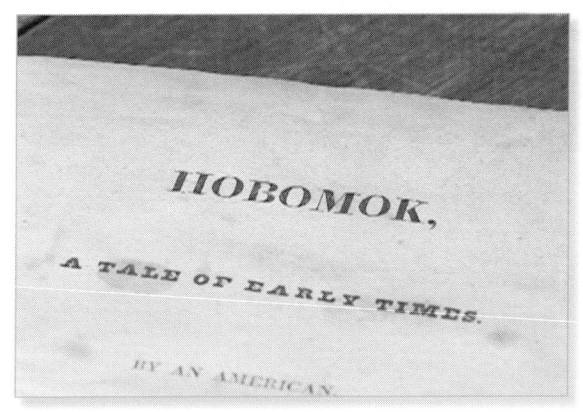

Hobomok inside front cover
(Wayland Historical Society)

Illustrations page 1

OVER THE RIVER...LIFE OF LYDIA MARIA CHILD

David Lee Child, 1828 (Library of Congress)

Illustrations page 2

HISTORIC IMAGES

African-American Woman with White Child (Roger Harvey)

Illustrations page 3

William Lloyd Garrison at 30-years-old
(Library of Congress)

HISTORIC IMAGES

Slave Punishment (Library of Congress)

Illustrations page 5

Attack on the Post Office (Library of Congress)

HISTORIC IMAGES

Indian Congress (Library of Congress)

Nat Turner Slave Rebellion
(Library of Congress)

Illustrations page 7

OUTRAGE.

Fellow Citizens,

AN

ABOLITIONIST,

of the most revolting character is among you, exciting the feelings of the North against the South. A seditious Lecture is to be delivered

THIS EVENING,

at 7 o'clock, at the Presbyterian Church in Cannon-street.
You are requested to attend and unite in putting down and silencing by peaceable means this tool of evil and fanaticism.
Let the rights of the States guaranteed by the Constitution be protected.

Feb. 27, 1837.   *The Union forever!*

Outrage by Proslavers of the North (Library of Congress)

HISTORIC IMAGES

British Abolitionist, George Thompson
(Library of Congress)

Illustrations page 9

James Forten
(Library of Congress)

HISTORIC IMAGES

American Colonization Society Warehouse (Library of Congress)

Illustrations page 11

Abolition Frowned Down
(Gag Rule Suppression)
(Library of Congress)

Ellen and William Craft
(Library of Congress)

HISTORIC IMAGES

Monks and Nuns:
The Status of Women in Ancient Religion
(Library of Congress)

Illustrations page 13

Sarah Parker Remond, Abolitionist
(Library of Congress)

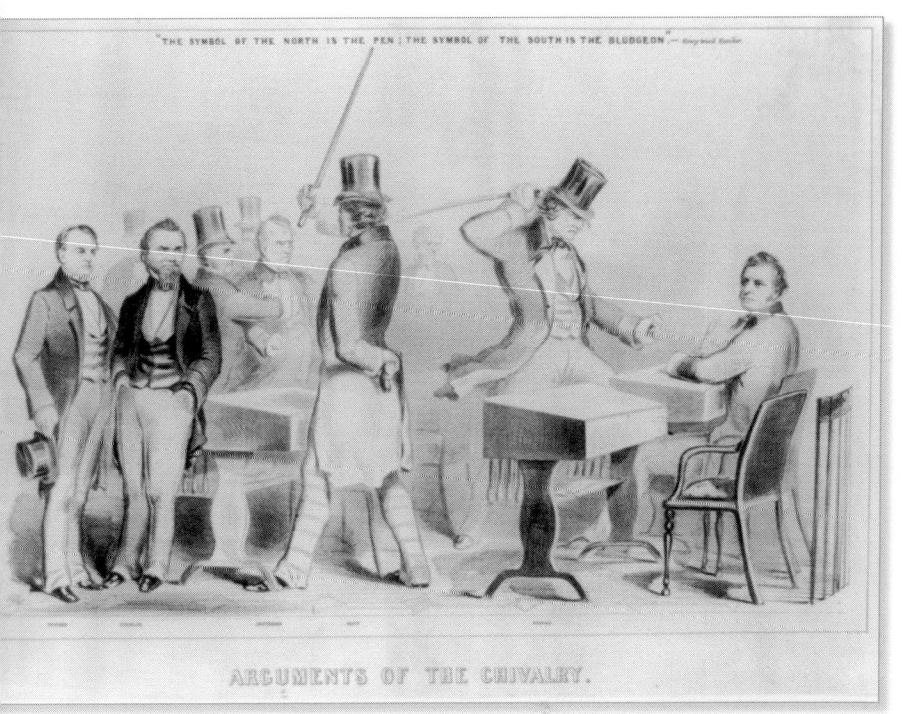

HISTORIC IMAGES

Caning of MA Senator, Charles Sumner
(Library of Congress)

Illustrations page 15

Over the River...Life of Lydia Maria Child

Martial Law/Negro Exodus (Library of Congress)

Illustrations page 16

HISTORIC IMAGES

Dred Scott of the Dred Scott Decision of 1857
(Library of Congress)

Illustrations page 17

John Brown (Library of Congress)

Historic Images

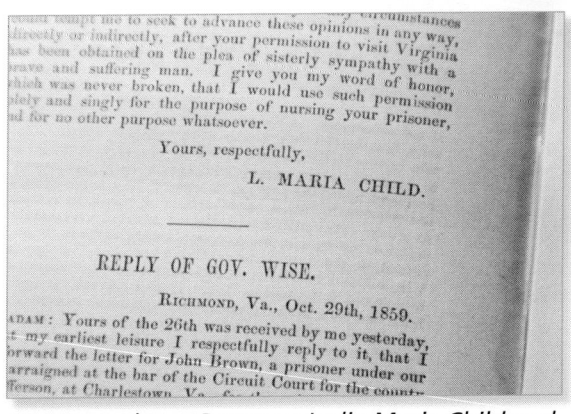

Correspondence Between Lydia Maria Child and Governor Wise and Mrs. Mason of Virginia
(Permanent Productions)

Illustrations page 19

Miscegenation Ball (Library of Congress)

HISTORIC IMAGES

John Brown (Library of Congress)

Illustrations page 21

New York Draft Riots (Conscription Act)
(Library of Congress)

Col. Robert G. Shaw of the 54th Black Regiment
MA State Capital Monument
(Permanent Productions)

OVER THE RIVER...LIFE OF LYDIA MARIA CHILD

African-American Children in the Classroom
(Library of Congress)

Illustrations page 24

HISTORIC IMAGES

Lydia Maria Child on the porch (1865) the year
Civil War ended
(Library of Congress)

Illustrations page 25

Daguerreotype of Lydia Maria Child (1856)
(Library of Congress)

Illustrations page 26

HISTORIC IMAGES

Older African-American man and woman sitting at table (Library of Congress)

Illustrations page 27

Older David Child, 1870 (Library of Congress)

Historic Images

U.S. Congress, 1830s (Library of Congress)

Illustrations page 29

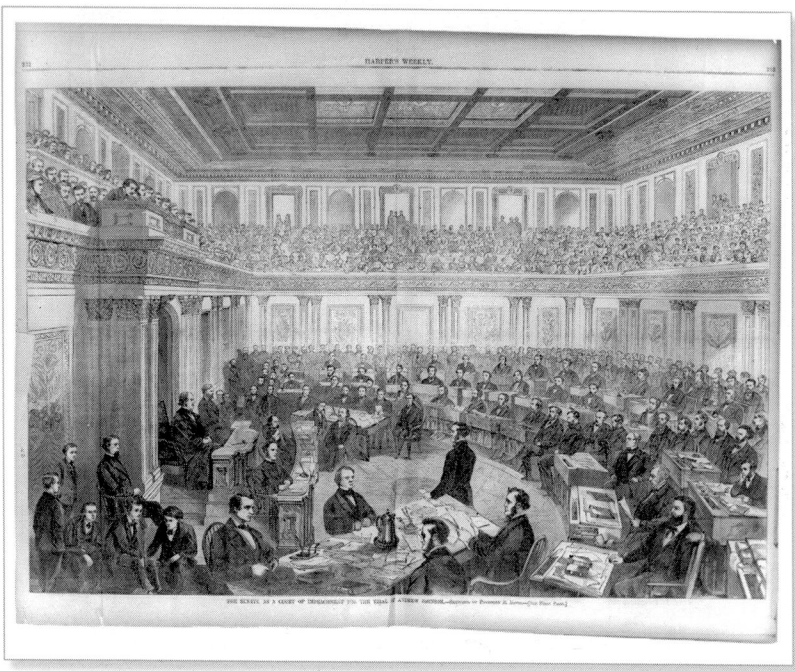

U.S. Congress 1866 (Library of Congress)

Illustrations page 30

HISTORIC IMAGES

Lydia Maria Child Portrait (1865)
Wayland Public Library, MA

Illustrations page 31

Chapter Four

More Congressional Infighting / Moral Repulsion Of Slavery & Maria's Deep Depression

The so-called "Compromise of 1850" was not really a true concession from both sides, although it did abolish the slave trade, not slavery itself, in the District of Columbia. Its worst feature was a tough new statute that went far beyond the 1793 Fugitive Slave Law. The Fugitive Slave Act of 1850 allowed anyone to claim a black as a slave and gave federal commissioners the authority to control a black person's fate without the benefit of a jury trial or testimony by the accused. A further provision, which left uncertainty on whether the spread of slavery would continue, allowed any state that came into the Union a choice to enter with or without slavery. Texas was admitted as a slave state and California, a free state. Finally, the new fugitive slave act empowered federal marshals to force all citizens to aid in recapturing fugitives or risk fines up to $1,000 and imprisonment for up to 6 months.

Abolitionists immediately started violating the tyrannical law and began harboring runaway slaves such as Ellen and William Craft, the famous couple whose fair-skinned wife cross-dressed as a male slave owner and escaped with her dark-skinned husband dressed as a servant. Slave catching became a profitable business under the new fugitive slave law of 1850—but a risky business. In reversed aggression, the captors risked being mobbed by abolitionists, sued for false imprisonment, or prosecuted for kidnapping. Sensing the tension brewing, Maria wrote to her Quaker friends, the Carpenters:

> "There seems to be a lull in fugitive slave matters. What experiment our masters will try next remains to be shown. The commercial and moneyed portion of the community will, doubtless, obey their orders to any extent. But in the heart of the people, I think a better and braver sentiment is gradually being formed. A friend of mine in Medford sheltered a fugitive a short time ago. When the firemen of the town heard of it, they sent for the man chattel, elected him a member of their company, and promised, at a given signal, to rally for his defense in case he was pursued and to stand by him to death, one and all."
>
> **Lydia Maria Child**

Maria's literary career had come to a standstill. She was approaching 50, and David was approaching 60. She wrote to her friends, the Lorings, asking for financial support:

Chapter Four: More Congressional Infighting

> "Everything has gone against David, as usual. For two months, he has been very ill and weak. He has had a bad fall. The outgoes have been much more than I expected—the income will be less. I work hard and practice a degree of economy which pinches my soul 'til I despite its smallness. Even if I had time to write, all power of thinking, and still more of imagining, is pressed out of me by this perpetual load of anxiety. I must rely upon you, my dear friend, to help me through the dark hours."
>
> Lydia Maria Child

While Maria was strapped in debt and deeply depressed about it, Harriet Beecher Stowe wrote a series of stories for the abolitionist newspaper, the *National Era*, from June 1851 to March 1852, when it finally appeared as a novel titled, *Uncle Tom's Cabin*—this was a novel about the heartbreaks slaves endured as they were routinely sold away from their loved ones, often to face brutal treatment on the cotton plantations of the Deep South. Within a year, 300,000 copies were sold in the United States. In the wake of the Civil War, the American and British sales were in the millions, and people all over the world read it in 40 translations. Many had expected Maria to be the first to write such a novel. Maria, in 1852, was called to her dear friend, Isaac Hopper's deathbed. She promised to write his biography. Isaac's biography was partly in defense of his radical Quaker views, and it also gave anecdotes of his long life of social service. Beloved by many, *Isaac T. Hopper, a*

True Life, stayed in print for over 30 years, yet it was still the only thing she wrote in a while. Maria reflected on her life and wrote to the Lorings:

> "I have never been so much depressed in spirits. You talk of my being a saint of the 19th century. Alas, I am poorly calculated for it now. The experience of the last eight years has terribly shaken my faith in human nature; however, I will try to do the best I can with what remains of my once strong and electric nature. Resignation to life is all I now aim at or hope for. My external relations are too much at war with my interior life. I give up the long-contested battle and surrender myself prisoner."
>
> **Lydia Maria Child**

Maria Publishes a Pioneering First: *The Progress of Religious Ideas*

In a deep depression, Maria almost relinquished her hard-won independence. Once again, Maria found writing to be her armory against insanity. She published in 1855 *The Progress of Religious Ideas*. It was her association with Isaac Hopper that spawned her ideas in *The Progress*. Isaac Hopper had played an active part in two controversies over slavery that had bitterly divided the Quaker community. Observing the schism between orthodox and Hicksite Friends in the 1820s and the expulsion of active abolitionists, among them Isaac Hopper, she witnessed the Quakers' betrayal of their anti-slavery heritage, which Maria

Chapter Four: More Congressional Infighting

attributed to their increasing prosperity, a pattern she had noted in every religious group she had studied, including the primitive Christians.

Like so many of Maria's literary contributions, *The Progress of Religious Ideas* was a pioneering first. The book encompassed all of the major religions of the ancient world, showing them in their own light, examining their beauty and their blemishes with complete impartiality, favoring none of them. In combating sectarianism and intolerance toward non-Christian religions, Maria repeatedly urged readers to consider the point-of-view of the peoples whose faith were being assailed by Christian proselytizers. Maria also focused on the issue of slavery since pro-slavery apologists and abolitionists debated whether or not the Bible sanctioned the peculiar institution. Her other focus was on the status of women under the various religions of the ancient world. The book met with strong criticism from reviewers, who accused Maria of bias against Christianity.

> "Child had nowhere acknowledged the divine origin and authority of Christianity which left room for inference that the incarnation and trinity of the Hindus stand on about the same level as the corresponding article of the Christian faith."
>
> **Religious Critic**

In reflecting back on her career, Maria drew an analogy between *The Progress of Religious Ideas* and the *Appeal. An Appeal* had sought to liberate Americans from the shackles of racial bigotry—the latter from the shackles of religious bigotry.

Moral Repulsion Over the Spread of Slavery into the West
The Gag Rule had ended in Congress by 1844, and moral repulsion of slavery by 1856 had taken a hold of the northern conscience, but, still, slavery continued. The rapid growth of slavery in Missouri prior to the U.S. Civil War exceeded the number of slaves available to sustain the economy there. In desperation for supply, values for slaves rose, and the acquisition of slaves were in high demand. Civil war between pro-slavery and anti-slavery settlers in Kansas broke out in 1855 as a result of the Kansas/Nebraska Act allowing for the expansion of slavery anywhere in the United States. The spread of slavery and the cancerous growth of the slave power continued to fuel Maria's indignation. Early in the election campaign for president in 1856, a Buffalo, New York, Republican wrote to Senator William Seward, sensing that the public opinion was, he said, "... on the tiptoe of revolution." But in all it appeared, the Southern Democratic Party was still in charge.

The Republican Party was primarily composed of northern anti-slavery recruits who all shared in the belief that slavery represented a relic of barbarism—that if allowed to continue spreading, would block the advancement of free labor, squelch American prosperity, and degrade the status of the majority of ordinary citizens.

Political tension had finally boiled over. On May 22, 1856, following a two-day fiery speech delivered by Massachusetts Senator Charles Sumner denouncing the crimes against Kansas, South Carolina Congressman Preston Brooks, avenging an insult to the south, beat Sumner unconscious with a heavy gold-headed cane. The northern Republicans were galled by the south's behavior in the Senate chamber and by the westward movement of slavery.

Chapter Four: More Congressional Infighting

Even Maria, who had a disdain for politicians, cherished Charles Sumner as a model statesman of uncompromising integrity. Still recovering from the terrible blows that cracked his skull, Senator Sumner, thinking of Maria fondly, sent her flower seeds. She wrote to him:

> "When I received news, my first impulse was to rush directly to Washington to ascertain whether I could not supply to you, in some small degree, the absence of a mother's or sister's care. Had I not been tied to the bedside of my aged father, I verily believe I should have done it. My heart has bled so freely for suffering Kansas. I have felt such burning indignation at the ever-increasing insults and outrages of the south and the cold, selfish indifference of the north."
>
> Lydia Maria Child

Maria's long letter to Sumner praised his speech and condemned the north's spineless indifference to slavery:

> "I confess that my peace principles are sorely tried, insomuch that nothing suits my mood so well as Joan of Arc's floating banner and consecrated sword."
>
> Lydia Maria Child

Maria ended her letter to him:

> "You are present to my mind every hour in the day, and all my thoughts of you are baptized with blessings. May God and good angels guard you and restore your precious health."
>
> **Lydia Maria Child**

A couple of days later, Maria wrote to her friends in Medford, Lucy and Mary Osgood:

> "I have always dreaded civil war and prayed that it might be averted, but if there is no other alternatives than the endurance of such insults and outrages, I am resigned to its approach. One would think that the shallowest statesman might have foreseen that two such antagonistic elements as freedom and slavery could not long coexist in the same government."
>
> **Lydia Maria Child**

The climate of violence, the attacks on anti-slavery settlers, and the Civil War in Kansas motivated Maria to publish in 1856 a story, *The Kansas Immigrants* in the *New York Tribune* and also inspired her to write a song titled, *Song for the Free Soil Men*. In *The Kansas Immigrants*, Maria, for the first time, publicly advocated the right of women to vote. In addition to her literary contributions, Maria organized a sewing circle in Wayland, Massachusetts, to ship clothes and household items to the anti-slavery settlers in Kansas. David and Maria, in their old age, put all the energy they could muster into helping to resolve the Kansas crisis.

Chapter Four: More Congressional Infighting

"There is nothing I abhor like politics. I believe the devil has no other snare to be compared to it for drawing honest souls out of a straightforward line into all manner of serpent-like sinuosities."

Lydia Maria Child

"Free Soil ! Free Speech !, Free Men ! Fremont!"

Seeing politics as a necessary evil, she and David rallied around John C. Fremont, who vowed to prevent the expansion of slavery if he were elected president. The acclaimed "First Woman in the Republic" demonstrated why she had received such an ennobling title. Maria encouraged the male readers of *The Kansas Immigrants* to bring the women into the social fold as equal partners. The women of Kansas had been taking an active role in the struggle, and Maria recognized the impact they were making. Maria included a letter to the women of Kansas in the box of clothes her sewing circle sent. It was published in the Kansas free-soiler newspaper, *The Herald of Freedom*. In the process of realizing the significant changes that were going on with women on the front lines of abolitionism and suffrage, Maria re-evaluated the choices she had made in the past.

Lori Kenschaft:

> "So she fought from then on to let women have control of their own financial futures, and I think another way to think about her is as an old-style small guard Republican who believed very strongly in the importance of work—that everybody should have worthy work—that doesn't have to mean high status work or high prestige work but work that's worthy that contributes to the community and that is properly renumerated—that all the things she was trying to do was to enable everybody to have

Chapter Four: More Congressional Infighting

satisfying work and to be properly—not richly—but properly rewarded for it.

By 1856, women suffragists' message on equal rights was building momentum, influencing women's self-image, like Maria's, but Maria's public energies remained with abolishing slavery, though women suffrage leaders such as her dear friend, Lucretia Mott, used Maria's book, *The History of the Condition of Women*, to help promote their cause.

Living in Wayland, Massachusetts, with her dying father, the Childs were able to finally cut some of their expenses. The strained relationship between David and Maria's father turned into affection in their old age. The three had finally bonded. Unfortunately for the woman who had written the Thanksgiving Day poem turned song, *Over the River and Through the Woods to Grandmother's House We Go*, her father died on that joyful holiday in 1856. Maria wrote to her friend, Sarah Shaw, Robert Shaw's mother:

> "Yes, my beloved friend, the old man has gone home—always the dreary void. The old man loved me, and you know how foolishly my nature craves love. Never again can I be so important to any human being as I was to him. Always when I came back from Boston, there was a bright firelight in his room for me, and his hand was eagerly stretched out, and the old face lighted up as he said, 'You're welcome back, Maria.' This time when I came home, it was all dark and silent."
>
> **Lydia Maria Child**

To make emotional matters worse, a year and a half later, Maria's surrogate husband, legal adviser and beloved friend, Ellis Gray Loring, suddenly died at the age of 55.

Chapter Five

Secession Looming/ John Brown's Raid/ Maria's Resurgence

To add to the fuel of the civil war in Missouri and the cane beating of Senator Sumner, the Supreme Court's Dred Scott Decision of 1857 ruled that any laws restricting the spread of slavery, or the right of masters to bring slaves into free states, was unconstitutional. It also declared that only white persons could be U.S. citizens and that blacks had no rights which the white man was bound to respect. The increasing anti-slavery sentiment coincided with Maria's second wind of reform.

After almost 16 years of estrangement from the New England anti-slavery societies, in 1859, the Childs attended the convention where the abolitionist soldier, John Brown, was present. Maria did not hear the words of John Brown when he stalked out of the convention room after appealing to his fellow reformers:

> "Talk, talk, talk! That will never set the slave free! What is needed is action—action!"
>
> **John Brown**

Maria never met John Brown, although David did. She later realized that John Brown was hovering around her niece's husband, George Luther Stearns, and five other men later known as the Secret Six, some of them her friends. Unbeknownst to her, Brown was at the convention to collect money to be used to raid Harper's Ferry in hopes of creating a massive southern insurrection by the slaves. Later that year, his ill-fated raid failed but not for everyone. John Brown was captured, tried for treason, and scheduled for hanging in Virginia.

As a reaction to the imprisonment of John Brown, Maria thrust herself into the middle of the controversy when she wrote to John Brown offering to nurse his wounds and then wrote to Governor Wise of Virginia, requesting his assistance to allow her passage to nurse the battered Brown. Governor Wise responded with a southern gentleman's diatribe that he felt would be a propaganda victory, including admonishing Maria for appearing to be surprised by Brown's actions when she was just as guilty of Brown as, in his words:

> "...having whetted knives of butchery for our mothers, sisters, daughters, and babes."
>
> **Governor Henry Wise**

Wise then sent the correspondence to northern and southern newspapers. Governor Wise underestimated Maria Child. Maria wasted no time in gaining advantage in the battle to win over public opinion. She promptly sent an explanatory letter to the *New York Tribune* accompanied by an answer she had received from John Brown. Both of the letters had presented Brown and his abolitionist supporters, not as blood-thirsty fanatics, but as unassuming level-headed good Samaritans. Maria's private offer to nurse John Brown ended up attracting as much notoriety as Brown's interrogation interview that was reprinted, and it served the anti-slavery cause almost as effectively. Her audience then multiplied tenfold nationwide. When Margarita Mason, wife of Virginia Senator James Mason, sent a letter to Maria and also published it in the *Virginian Press*, it opened with:

> "Do you read your Bible, Mrs. Child? If you do, read there: 'Woe unto you, hypocrites.'"
> **Mrs. Margarita Mason of Virginia**

She went on to accuse Maria of:

> "...ignoring the objects of charity on your doorstep—the northern poor whites—and confining your sympathy to a man who had sought to unleash a servile war against the men, women, and children of your own race."
> **Mrs. Margarita Mason of Virginia**

Like Governor Wise, Mrs. Mason did not realize that she had written to the most skillful propagandist in the abolitionist movement. Maria submitted an 11-page answer to Mrs. Mason to the abolitionist editor, Horace Greeley, of the *New York Tribune*. Taking her cue from Mrs. Mason, Maria began with an array of Biblical text—18 quotations defending an anti-slavery interpretation of Christianity compared to the 2 Mrs. Mason had cited for pro-slavery purposes. Maria methodically tore apart Mrs. Mason's defense of slavery and exposed the absurdity of portraying slave-owning women as models of Christian charity, who stayed up all night taking care of dying slaves, helping slave mothers through childbirth, and sewing dresses for motherless slave children:

> "New England women, too, watched with the sick, sewed for the poor, and assisted in childbirth, but we pay our domestics generous wages with which they can purchase as many gowns as they please, and here at the north, after we have helped the mothers, we do not sell the babies."
> **Lydia Maria Child**

In the end, Maria publicly condoned violence to free the slaves:

> "In this enlightened age, all despotisms ought to come to an end by the agency of moral and rational means, but if they resist such agencies, it is in the order of providence that they must come to an end by violence."
> **Lydia Maria Child**

All three exchanges of the letters were compiled in an anti-slavery tract called *Correspondence Between Lydia Maria Child and Governor Wise and Mrs. Mason of Virginia*. Over 300,000 copies were sold throughout the United States and abroad, furthering Maria's social impact. The south's retaliation went beyond John Brown. Arrest warrants went out to

Senator Charles Sumner, Horace Greeley, some members of the Secret Six, and whomever the south deemed co-conspirators. Even the famous black abolitionist Frederick Douglass was implicated. She wrote to an abolitionist friend in praise of John Brown:

> "His failure is a most signal success and all owing to the simple greatness of his character. He speaks from an eminence none of us have reached, and he has the whole United States for an audience. Whether he lives or dies, he will shake the rotten institution to its foundation."
> **Lydia Maria Child**

Ralph Waldo Emerson wrote to Maria of his concerns of John Brown being put to death:

"I have hopes for his brave life. He is one for whom miracles wait."
Ralph Waldo Emerson

To be with her anti-slavery comrades, Maria went to Boston's Tremont Temple and helped her old friend, William Lloyd Garrison, arrange a commemorative centerpiece of John Brown in preparation for his memorial. The two old apostles recalled their pioneering days in the movement as they decorated the platform with many American civil and spiritual slogans.

On December 2, 1859, John Brown was executed. At the hour of John Brown's hanging, church bells tolled throughout America. Northerners gathered in many cities to pay tribute. Garrison spoke to thousands gathered at the temple:

> "As a peace man, I am prepared to say, 'Success to every slave insurrection at the south and in every slave country.' Rather than see men wearing their chains in a cowardly and servile spirit, I would, as an advocate of peace, much rather see them breaking the head of the tyrant with their chains."
>
> William Lloyd Garrison

Knowing that a civil war was looming, when Maria wrote of the women of the south, she expressed compassion for what may be ahead for them—the dread of a war:

> "After all, I have compassion for the people in Virginia, especially the women. If they could only see that their insecurity is owing to the hateful institution they cherish so blindly. Slavery or freedom must die, and the death grapple is close at hand. God, speed the right."
>
> Lydia Maria Child

Northern sympathies for the south, even among the moderate abolitionists, were now echoing throughout the presses, attacking Garrison and his so-called radical cohorts.

Aging Maria Continues Her Push to Abolish Slavery/ Secession & Civil War Looming

In Maria's old age, she became more radical. Living in Wayland, Massachusetts, she continued her anti-slavery work by publishing tracts, like the *Patriarchal Institution* and *The Duty of Disobedience to the Fugitive Slave Act*, of which she sent

CHAPTER FIVE: SECESSION LOOMING

copies to the newly-elected Massachusetts legislators. She also edited and wrote the preface of the first female slave narrative, *Incidents in the Life of a Slave Girl,* written by the fugitive slave, Harriet Jacobs, using a pseudonym of Linda Brent. Maria embraced Harriet as her protégé and praised her work as an added bonus to the cause because it appealed to the emotions of many who ignored the sexual brutality that existed in the south. Armored with God as her protector, Maria continued to attend anti-slavery meetings that were mobbed repeatedly by conservatives.

Compromise after compromise was presented to prevent secession. Northern Republicans, like Senator William Seward, offered a number of compromises to the south. Maria distrusted Seward, believing that he was ready to sell out completely to the south. Once an eloquent opponent of slavery, Seward had dropped his abolitionist rhetoric while angling for the Republican nomination, that went instead, to Abraham Lincoln. Maria commented of Seward:

> "When the presidency touches the hem of a man's garment, all virtue goes out of him."
> **Lydia Maria Child**

Abraham Lincoln was elected President of the United States. Threats from the south to secede and threats on Lincoln loomed before his victory. Finally, on December 20, 1860, South Carolina seceded. Maria wrote to her friend, Frances Shaw:

> "Alas, I am sorry to say I have more hope in the southern arrogance and rashness than I have in northern courage and conscientiousness. My hope is that the south will scorn to accept any compromise that the north will get on her knees to offer. The crisis must come, and, it seems to me, there can never be a time more favorable than the present."
>
> Lydia Maria Child

In June of 1861, Maria wrote to her friend, Sarah Shaw:

> "Civil war is an awful thing, and we cannot possibly foresee what is to be the end of it. I suppose no sane person doubts that the north must eventually beat, but after we conquered them, what are we to do with subjects whose character is so incongruous to ours and who hate us, our institutions, and our manners with such an irreconcilable hatred? We are on top of a giant wave, and it must drift us withersoever He wills."
>
> Lydia Maria Child

Maria ended her letter to Sarah with sympathies toward the slaves:

> "Oh, the poor slaves have so few friends and so many enemies. In all this war, there seems to be no feeling for them."
>
> Lydia Maria Child

Chapter Five: Secession Looming

The war brought unity among the anti-slavery factions, and Maria continued writing letters and making appearances at meetings and parties, where the mood always shifted to the war. Maria published more anti-slavery works and became involved with sending money and supplies to the abolitionist-led regiments and to the slaves who fled to the Union army lines. The Lincoln administration had now abandoned its policy of sending fugitives back to their masters on the grounds that they were confiscated enemy property or contrabands.

By 1862, Maria's patience with Lincoln grew thin. Public pressure for Lincoln to emancipate all of the slaves ran high, with a constant barrage of letters to the president. Finally, President Lincoln issued the *Emancipation Proclamation* on January 1, 1863.

"Our insane prejudice against color is very gradually, but surely, give way before the emergencies of the time and the laudable conduct of the colored people. Colonel Shaw of the Massachusetts 54th is a friend of mine, a noble-hearted young gentleman who left wealth and luxury and a most happy home to serve his country in her hour of need."

Lydia Maria Child

In March of 1863, the Conscription Act made all men age 20 to 45 eligible for military service, except for the rich, who could buy their way out. By July of 1863, draft riots broke out in New York, lasting for four days. Offices and homes of abolitionists and Republicans were sacked. The Colored Orphan Asylum was burned, and many African Americans were lynched on the streets. The police and federal troops finally stopped the mob. Many of the rioters were Irish immigrant laborers who feared that with emancipation, the blacks would come north, lower wages, and take jobs from the whites.

On July 18, 1863, Colonel Robert Gould Shaw and his black troops perished in a suicidal attack on Fort Wagner in Charleston Harbor, leaving a legacy of black heroism and martyrdom. In a letter to Robert's mother, Sarah, after reading the headlines of his death:

> "Your darling Robert made the most of the powers and advantages God had given him by consecrating them to the defense of freedom and humanity. Such a son in the spirit world is worth 10 living here for themselves only."
>
> **Lydia Maria Child**

Maria Writes *The Freedmen's Book*

Preparing for the day they were all freed, Maria began writing *The Freedmen's Book*, a self-help and black history book for the freed people of the south. Maria was far ahead of her time in realizing that students can learn to read more easily when textbooks give them a sense of self-worth and pride in their identity.

The Fight to Abolish Slavery has Ended

On January 31, 1865, Maria and David lived to see the 13th Amendment enacted, abolishing slavery, unlike her brother, Convers, who died 2 years earlier.

On April 15, 1865, just five days after the Civil War ended, President Lincoln was assassinated. Maria wrote to her dear friend, Sarah Shaw:

> "...The assassination of our good president shocked and distressed me. The kind-hearted Abraham was certainly in danger of making too easy terms with the Rebels. Perhaps he has been removed that he might not defeat his own work and that another, better calculated to carry it to a safe and sure end might come into his place. I have all along said that nothing could happen which would shake my faith—that God was not going to destroy this nation but only to mold it anew for the performance of a great work in the world...."
>
> **Lydia Maria Child**

Chapter Six

A New Day for America? Reconstruction Policy—First Civil Rights Bill Passed in 1866

On December 29, 1865, William Lloyd Garrison declared that the abolitionists' mission had ended. Garrison discontinued the publication of the *Liberator* and urged antislavery societies to fold and shift their energies to aid the freed slaves. Senator Charles Sumner and reformers in the predominantly Republican Congress were instrumental in drafting the Reconstruction Policy (the first Civil Rights Bill Passed in 1866). Maria and many of the great abolitionist leaders were now in advisory capacities, administering education societies and Freedmen's Aid Commissions.

Lincoln's successor, President Andrew Johnson, along with his congressional block of Confederate allies and conservative Republicans, thwarted many of the progressive Reconstruction programs. Johnson pardoned many of the Confederate Rebels, approved state- enacted Black Codes, vetoed the bill extending the Freedmen's Bureau, and took over the control of the

Reconstruction Policy. The freed people and abolitionist reformers realized that they had won the war, only to lose the peace.

To escape terror and oppression in the late 1870s, thousands of African Americans fled the south to find refuge in the north and west in what was called the Negro Exodus. The largest number went to Kansas.

Maria Child lived 15 years after the Civil War, burying David in 1874 and saying her last goodbyes to her dear friend, William Lloyd Garrison, before he died in 1879. In remembering the glory days and Garrison's importance, Maria wrote to a friend:

> "It is wonderful how one mortal may affect the destiny of a multitude. I remember very distinctly the first time I ever saw Garrison. I was then all absorbed in poetry and painting, soaring aloft on psyche wings into the ethereal regions of mysticism. He got hold of the strings of my conscience and pulled me into reforms. It is of no use to imagine what might have been if I had never met him. Old dreams vanished, old associates departed, and all things became new, but the new surroundings were all alive, and they brought a moral discipline worth 10 times the sacrifice they cost."
>
> **Lydia Maria Child**

Unofficially canonized by abolitionists as a saint for her sacrifice of fame and fortune to advocate on behalf of the oppressed people, she was credited with the divine power to create light out of darkness and bring a sinful nation to repentance. Maria gained icon status equal to Garrison's in the memories of the abolitionist family. An excerpted tribute by Reverend Henry Ludlow captured the impact Maria had on the world around her:

> "One Mrs. Child has done more to wake up the people to effort in this cause of God and humanity than all the men that went before her in this country."
>
> **Reverend Henry Ludlow**

In one of her last letters to her dear friends, the Shaws, Maria wrote about her sympathy for the freed people in their exodus and their enduring suffering, but she still saw hope:

> "Notwithstanding the miserable blunders of our government and the abominable knavery of politicians, there has been a great gain. They cannot be bought and sold in the market, they can emigrate, and we have made no contract to send them back. Best of all, there is now a possible basis for the salutary education of both races."
>
> **Lydia Maria Child**

Rest in Peace, Maria

On October 20, 1880, Lydia Maria Child, the great abolitionist for freedom, died, peacefully, in her home, in Wayland, Massachusetts. Her Will continued her altruistic endeavors. Her legacy embodies the best of the American heritage. Lydia Maria Francis Child's heroic commitment to the vision of a culturally pluralistic America with equal rights and opportunity for all and her bravery in the face of obstacles, danger, poverty, and defeats, challenge us to follow her example:

> "I long for the time to come when men will realize that all races are children of the same Father and that all, according to the degrees of light they have, are feeling after God, if happily they may find Him."
>
> **Lydia Maria Child**

Acknowledgements

Many thanks to Milton Meltzer, Patricia Holland, and Francine Drasno whose book *Lydia Maria Child Selected Letters, 1817-1880* contributed to the documentary and this book.

Kudos and gratitude to the leading Maria Child historian, Carolyn L. Karcher, who tediously combed through microfilm and archives to publish the world-renowned book, *The First Woman in the Republic* which greatly contributed to the understanding of Lydia Maria Child's private and public self. I'd like to extend my appreciation of her for reviewing the script and guiding me in this wonderful endeavor.

Much appreciation to other Lydia Maria Child biographers for their contributions to this book and documentary: Deborah Clifford, Lori Kenschaft, and Bruce Mills.

Special thanks to the biographers whose books on America during the 18th and 19th Century helped in compiling "the times."

Special love goes out to the many thousands of anti-slavery warriors of the 18th and 19th century in America who made freedom possible.

Lastly, much gratitude and love to my partner, Michele Patterson who was quite patient with me and even enjoyed hearing me go on and on about how ennobling Lydia Maria Child was. Now she is a believer. Thank you Michele, for your assistance in making the documentary and this book have wings.

Illustrations Credits

1. Frontispiece Young Lydia Maria Child, 1826 (Library of Congress)
2. *Juvenile Miscellany* (Wayland Historical Society)
3. *Hobomok* inside front cover (Wayland Historical Society)
4. David Lee Child, 1828 (Library of Congress)
5. African-American Woman with White Child (Roger Harvey)
6. William Lloyd Garrison at 30-years-old (Library of Congress)
7. Slave Punishment (Library of Congress)
8. Attack on the Post Office (Library of Congress)
9. Indian Congress (Library of Congress)
10. Nat Turner Slave Rebellion (Library of Congress)
11. Outrage by Proslavers of the North (Library of Congress)
12. George Thompson (Library of Congress)
13. James Forten (Library of Congress)
14. ACS Warehouse (Library of Congress)
15. Abolition Frowned Down (Gag Rule Suppression) (Library of Congress)
16. Ellen and William Craft (Library of Congress)
17. Monks and Nuns (Library of Congress)
18. Sarah Parker Remond (Library of Congress)
19. Caning of MA Senator, Charles Sumner (Library of Congress)
20. Martial Law/Negro Exodus (Library of Congress)
21. Dred Scott of the Dred Scott Decision of 1857 (Library of Congress)
22. John Brown (Library of Congress)
23. *Correspondence Between Lydia Maria Child and Governor Wise and Mrs. Mason of Virginia* (Permanent Productions)
24. Miscegenation Ball (Library of Congress)
25. John Brown (Library of Congress)

26. New York Draft Riots (Conscription Act) (Library of Congress)
27. Col. Robert Shaw of the 54th Black Regiment MA State Capital Monument (Permanent Productions)
28. African-American Children in the Classroom (Library of Congress)
29. Lydia Maria Child on the porch (1865) the year Civil War ended.
30. Daguerreotype of Lydia Maria Child (1856) (Library of Congress)
31. Older African-American Man and woman sitting at table (Library of Congress)
32. Older David Child, 1870 (Library of Congress)
33. U.S. Congress, 1830s (Library of Congress)
34. U.S. Congress 1866 (Library of Congress)
35. Lydia Maria Child Portrait (1865) Wayland Public Library, MA

Books About Lydia Maria Child

Kenschaft, Lori. *Lydia Maria Child: The Quest for Racial Justice.* New York: Oxford University Press, 2002.

Karcher, Carolyn L., ed. *A Lydia Maria Child Reader.* Durham: Duke University Press, 1997.

Mills, Bruce. *Cultural Reformations: Lydia Maria Child and the Literature of Reform.* Athens: University of Georgia Press, 1994.

Karcher, Carolyn L. *The First Woman in the Republic: A Cultural Biography of Lydia Maria Child.* Durham: Duke University Press, 1994.

Clifford, Deborah Pickman. *Crusader for Freedom: A Life of Lydia Maria Child.* Boston: Beacon Press, 1992.

Meltzer, Milton, Patricia G. Holland, and Francine Drasno, eds. *Lydia Maria Child: Selected Letters, 1817-1880.* Amherst: University of Massachusetts Press, 1982.

Meltzer, Milton. *Tongue of Flame: The Life of Lydia Maria Child.* New York: Crowell, 1965.

Baer, Helene G. *The Heart is Like Heaven: The Life of Lydia Maria Child.* Philadelphia: University of Pennsylvania Press, 1964.

Index

illus. p2 refers to page 2 of the illustration pages.

A

Abenaki Indians, xiii
abolition frowned down, illus. p12
abolitionist movement
    An Appeal, influence of, 35, xiv, xv
    Child as propagandist, 35, 67, xxv
    disagreement within, 44
    Higginson, Thomas W., 13, xxv
    women and, 39
abolitionist newspaper, 55, xvi
abolitionists
    Alcott, Louisa May, xxv
    An Appeal, influence of, 35–36, xiv
    Annual, 51
    Beecher, Lyman, 9
    Beecher Stowe, Harriet, 5, 55, xxv
    Brown, John, 65–70, illus. p18, p21
    canonization of Maria Child, 78
    Carpenters, 54
    Child, Lydia Maria, 78, 81, xiv, xvi
    Conscription Act, reaction to, 75
    Craft, Ellen and William, 54
    Douglass, Frederick, 69, xxv
    Emerson, Ralph Waldo, 37, 69, xxv
    Forten, James, 18
    Francis, Convers Jr., 5
    Freedmen's Aid Commissions, 77
    Garrison, William Lloyd, 2, 32, 35, 38, 70, 77–78, xiv
    Greeley, Horace, 67, 69
    Grimke, Angelina, 42
    Hicksite Friends, 56
    Higginson, Thomas Wentworth, 13, xxv
    home and offices, sacking of, 75
    Hopper, Isaac and Hannah, 46, 56
    Juvenile Miscellany (Child), 13

Kelley, Abby, 43
Liberator, 24, 32–34, 46, 77
literary figures, xv
May, Reverend Samuel, 32
meetings, storming of, 38
Moore, John, 20
National Anti-Slavery Standard, 51, xvi, xviii, xxi
National Era, 55
northern, 40, 70
offices, vandalized, 38
opinions, different, 45
public sanctions, 38
radical, 28, 70, xiv
Reconstruction Policy, 78
regiments, 73
runaway slaves, harbouring, 53–54
Seward, William, 58–60, 71
sheltering of Maria and David, 41
slavery, Biblical sanctioned, 57
southern, 40
Sumner, Senator Charles, 58–60, 65, 69, 77, illus. p15
Thompson, George, 38–39
Thoughts on African Colonization (Garrison), 32
white, 32
Worcester, Thomas, 8
ACS. *See* American Colonization Society (ACS)
Adams, Hannah, 34
Adams, John Quincy, 20, 27
African-American
    children in classroom, illus. p24
    community, 18, 21, 29, 75
    man and woman, illus. p27
    myth of African inferiority, 25
    troops, heroism of, xvi
    Woman with White Child, illus. p3
Alabama, 19

INDEX

Alcott, Louisa May, xxv
Alton Observer, 40
American Colonization Society (ACS), 17–18, 20, 22–23, 32, illus. p11
American Constitution, 4, 17, 22
American Revolution, 2, 14
Annual, 51
anti-miscegenation laws, xxvi
anti-slavery
   activism, 35
   appeals, 29
   articles, 40, 43
   books, 34–35, 38, xxv–xxvi
   cause/work, 35, 67, 70, 73
   Christian interpretation, 67
   editorials, 46
   factions, 73
   fair, 34
   gift book, xxi
   leader, 40
   meetings, 41, 71
   movement, 8, 44–45
   newspapers, 30, 32, 49, 51, xxi
   northern recruits, 58
   organizations, 51
   propagandist, xxv
   Quaker heritage, 56
   radicals, 29
   sentiment, 65
   settlers, 58, 60
   short-story, 32, xx
   societies, 32, 34, 39, 45, 65
   stories, 41
Anti-Slavery Catechism (Child), 43, xxi
Appeal for the Indians, An (Child), xxii
Appeal in Favor of That Class of Americans Called Africans (Child), 34–36, 39, xiv, xv, xvi, xxi, xxv–xxvi
Appeal to the Christian Women of the Southern States, An (Grimke), 42
Appeal to the Colored Citizens of the World, An (Walker), 21–22
"Appeal to the Women of the Nominally Free States, An" (Child), 43, 57

aristocracy, 41–43
Arkansas, 19
Aspirations of the World. A Chain of Opals (Child), xvii, xxii
assimilation
   of blacks, 25
   of Native Americans, 11, 25, 27
   racial, 28
Atlantic Monthly, The, xxii
Autumnal Leaves (Child), xxi

B

Beecher, Lyman, 9
Beecher Stowe, Harriet, 5, 55, xxv
Belinda, 2
bigotry, racial and religious, 57, xvii, xix
Biographical Sketches of Great and Good Men (Child), xx
Biography of Lady Russell (Child), xx
Biography of Madame de Stael (Child), xx
Biography of Madame Guyon (Child), xx
Biography of Madame Roland (Child), xx
Black Codes, 77
"Black Saxons, The" (Child), xxi
black stereotypes, 25
Black Suffrage, xvi, xxii
Body of Liberties, 1
Boston Athenaeum, 34, xvi
Boston before the Revolution (Child), xv
Brahmin, xvii
British anti-slavery societies, 39
British West Indies, 38
Brooks, Preston, 58
Brown, John, 65–70, illus. p18, illus. p21
Bull, Ole, 46

C

Calhoun, John C., 18, 20
California, 53
capital punishment, xviii, xix
Carpenter, Margaret and Joseph, 52, 54
Catholicism, 41
Channing, William Ellery, 36
"Charity Bowery" (Child), xxi

89

Cherokee Indians, 27, xiv
Child, David Lee
  anti-slavery editorials, 46
  anti-slavery organization, 51
  beet farming, 43, 45
  death of, 78
  financially irresponsible, 16, 37–38
  libel suits and prison, 30, 39
  marriage to Maria Lydia Francis, 14–15, 27, 47, 52, 55, xiv
  Massachusetts Journal, 14, 25, 27, 29, 31
  pictures of, illus. p2, illus. p28
  Turner, Nat, 25
Child, Lydia Maria. *See also* Francis, Lydia Maria
  abolitionist *Annual,* 51
  abolitionist movement, 35
  abolitionist newspaper, 55, xvi
  anti-slavery articles, 40, 43
  anti-slavery books, 34–35, 38, xxv–xxvi
  anti-slavery cause/work, 35, 67
  anti-slavery fair, 34
  anti-slavery meetings, 41, 71
  anti-slavery organization, 51
  anti-slavery propagandist, 35, 67, xxv
  anti-slavery short stories, 32, xx
  anti-slavery stories, 41
  Antislavery Catechism, 43
  Appeal for the Indians, An, xxii
  Appeal in Favor of That Class of Americans Called Africans, 34–35, 39, xiv, xv, xvi, xxi, xxv–xxvi
  "Appeal to the Women of the Nominally Free States, An," 43, 57
  assimilation of blacks, 25
  assimilation of Native Americans, 25, 27
  black stereotypes, dismissed, 25
  Brown, John, 65–69
  canonization by abolitionists, 78

Carpenter, Margaret and Joseph, 52, 54
Comparative Strength of Male and Female Intellect, The, 30, xx
Correspondence Between Lydia Maria Child and Governor Wise and Mrs. Mason of Virginia, 68, xxii, illus. p19
Cure of Slavery, 43
David's debts, 21, 29, 43
death of, 81
death of David Child, 78
death of William Lloyd Garrison, 78
domestic advice book, 20–21
Duty of Disobedience to the Fugitive Slave Act, The, 70, xxii
economic freedom, loss of, 15, 29
emancipation of slaves, 5, 16, 30, 34, 44
father's death, 63
financial hardship from activism, 35
financial support from father, 11–12
First Settlers of New England, The, 27–28, xx
"First Woman in the Republic," 2, 31, 62
Fountain, The, 43
Free Inquirer, The, 30, 46
Freedmen's Book, The (Child), 75, xvi, xxii
Freemont, John C., 62
Frugal Housewife, The, 21, 35, 43, xv, xx
Grimke, Angelina, 42
"Hints to People of Moderate Fortune," 30
History of the Condition of Women, Authentic Anecdotes of American Slavery, 39, 63, xvii, xxi
Hobomok, a Tale of Early Times (Child), 11–12, xv, xx, illus. p1
Indian rights, 16
interracial marriage, 27
Isaac T. Hopper: A True Life, 55–56, xxi

Index

Child, Lydia Maria *(continued)*
   "Jumbo and Zairee," 32, xx
   Juvenile Miscellany magazine, 5, 12–13, 25, 27, 32, 43, xv, xx, xxviii–xxix, illus. p1
   "Kansas Emigrants, The," 60, xxi
   letter about Garrison, 78
   letter on mob violence, 44
   letter to Abby Kelley, 43–44
   letter to Charles Sumner, 59–60
   letter to Convers, 42
   letter to David, 38
   letter to Ellis Loring, 48, 55–56
   letter to Frances Shaw, 49, 71–72, 80
   letter to John Hopper, 48–49, 55
   letter to Maria Lowell, 49
   letter to Mary Preston, 15
   letter to Robert Shaw's mother, 75
   letter to Sarah Shaw, 63, 72, 76, 80
   letter to the Osgoods, 60
   letter to Virginians, 70
   "Letters from New York," 51, xxi
   Liberator, The, 46
   library privileges, 34, xvi
   Lincoln, President Abraham, 76
   Little Girl's Own Book, The, 21, xx
   "Maria," adoption of name, 9
   marriage to David Lee Child, 14–15, 27, 47, 52, 55, xiv
   Mason, Mrs. Margarita, 67–68
   Massachusetts Journal, 14, 27, 29–30, xx
   mob violence, letter on, 44
   moral answers in religion, 23
   Mother's Book, The, 21, 35, xv, xx
   Mott, Lucretia, 42
   National Anti-Slavery Standard, 51, xvi, xviii, xxi
   New York, move to, 51–52
   New York Courier, The, 46
   North American Review, 12, 34
   Oasis, The, 43
   obituary notices, xxv
   passion for knowledge, 7
   Patriarchal Institution, 70
   Philosophy and *Consistency,* 30
   Philothea, 36, xxi
   pictures of, ix, illus. p25–26, illus. p31
   Politeness, 30
   politics, dislike of, 61
   President, wrote to, 62, 73, xxix
   Progress of Religious Ideas, Through Successive Age, The (Child), 56–57, xvii, xxi
   property transfer to Ellis Loring, 50
   racial assimilation, 28
   racial equality, 34, xvi, xix, xxvi, xxvii
   Rebels, or Boston before the Revolution (1825), The, xv, xx
   relationship with Ellis Loring, 46–47, 50, 64
   relationship with John Hopper, 46–49
   relationship with Ole Bull, 46
   role model for women, 37, 39
   sewing circle, 60, 62
   "St. Domingo Orphans, The," 32, xx
   Standard, 45–46, 49, xviii, xxii, xxix
   Thanksgiving Day poem, 63, xxv
   tolerance, 11, 27, 57, xix, xxvi, xxvii
   violence to free slaves, 26, 68
   "What is Beauty?", 47
   white person promoting racial equality, xxvii
   women's equal rights with men, 37, 39–40, 62, xxviii, xxix
   women's suffrage movement, 60, 63, xxix
   "Year of the Mob," 38–40
"Chocorua's Curse" (Child), xx
Church in the Wilderness (Child), xx
Church of the New Jerusalem, 8
civil rights, xiv
Civil Rights Bill (1866), 77
Civil Rights movement, xix, xxvi
Civil War, 55, 58, 60, 72, 76, 78, xvi, xvii
Clay, Henry, 18, 20, 22–23
Clifford, Deborah, 37, 87, xxix
Colored Orphan Asylum, The, 75

Commonwealth of Massachusetts, 2
Comparative Strength of Male and Female Intellect, The (Child), 30, xx
"Compromise of 1850," 53
Confederate Rebels, 77
Connecticut, 2
Conscription Act (1863), 75, illus. p22
Constitution of the United States of America, 4, 17, 22
Correspondence Between Lydia Maria Child and Governor Wise and Mrs. Mason of Virginia, 68, xxii, illus. p19
Cottage Place, 38
cotton, 18–19, 55
Cotton Gin, 17
Craft, Ellen and William, 54, illus. p12
crime, xviii
Crusader for Freedom: A Life of Lydia Maria Child (Clifford), 87, xxix
Cuffee, Paul, 18
Cure of Slavery, The (Child), 43, xxi

D

Declaration of Independence, 4, 22
Deep South, 19, 55
Desire (ship), 1
Dial, The, 47
discrimination, xiv, xxvi
District of Columbia, 23, 33–34
Douglass, Frederick, 69, xxv
dowry system, 39
Dred Scott Decision (1857), 65, illus. p17
Duty of Disobedience to the Fugitive Slave Act, The (Child), 70, xxii

E

economic barriers, xix
education of former slaves, xvi
Electoral College delegations, 17
Emancipation Proclamation (1863), 73, vii
Emerson, Ralph Waldo, 37, 69, xxv
Emily Parker (Child), xx
employment bans, xxvi

Episcopalianism, 41
Evenings in New England (Child), xx
Evils of Slavery, The (Child), xxi

F

Family Nurse, The (Child), xxi
15th Amendment, xix
First Settlers of New England, The (Child), 27–28, xx
First Woman in the Republic, The (Karcher), 83, 87, xxvii
Florida, 19
Flowers, Ann, xxviii–xxix
Flowers for Children (Child), xxi
Fort Wagner (Charleston), 75
Forten, James, 18, illus. p10
Fountain, The (Child), 43
14th Amendment, xix
Francis, Benjamin, 2
Francis, Convers Jr.
  avid reader, 6
  death of, 76
  Maria, cautioned, 35
  Maria, rift with, 36, 40–42
  schooling, 7
  Transcendentalist, 5
  Unitarian minister, 5
Francis, Convers Sr., 1, 63
Francis, James, 5, 35
Francis, Lydia Maria. *See also* Child, Lydia Maria
  abolitionist, 13, xxviii
  anti-slavery movement, 8
  baptism by father, 9
  birth, 1, xiii
  blacks, oppression of, 4
  Calvinism, 7, 9
  childhood, 5–6
  doctrinal bigotry, xvii
  financial support by father, 11–12
  inalienable rights and freedom, 4
  interracial union, 12
  Juvenile Miscellany magazine, 5, 12–13, xv, xx, xxviii–xxix

literature appreciation, 7
moral principles, 5
mother's death, 5, xiii
"My Mother's Grave," 5
Native American, integration of, xxviii
Native American rights, 13
Native Americans, 11
Native Americans, oppression of, 4
North American Review, 12
passion for knowledge, 7
picture, ix
Rebels, A Tale of The Revolution, The, 14
Rebels, or Boston before the Revolution (1825), *The,* xv, xx
religion explorations, 7–8
religious tolerance, xvii
schooling, 6–7
sectarianism, challenged, xvii
social conscience, xvii
spiritual hunger, xvii
Swedenborgianism, 8
tolerance, racial and religious, 11
Unitarianism, 9
women, oppression of, 4
women's rights, 13
women's roles in society, 11
Francis, Susannah, 1, 5
Franklin, Benjamin, 31
Free Inquirer, The, 30, 46
free states, 20, 53, 65
freed people, 75, 78, 80, xvi
Freedmen's Aid Commissions, 77
Freedmen's Book, The (Child), 75, xvi, xxii
Freedmen's Bureau, 77
Freesoiler town, 1
Fremont, John C., 62
Frugal Housewife, The (Child), 21, 35, 43, xv, xx
Fugitive Slave Act (1850), 53
Fugitive Slave Law (1793), 53
Fuller, Margaret, 47, 51

G

Gag Rule, 40, 58, illus. p12
Garrison, William Lloyd
abolitionist leader, 2
abolitionists' mission, 77
ACS, dissenting against, 23
black stereotypes, dismissed, 25
Brown, John, 69–70
Clay, Henry, 23
death of, 78
England, trip for the Childs, 38
fiery style of, 36
Francis, Lydia, 2
Genius of Universal Emancipation, The, 30
Liberator (newspaper), 24, 32–34, 46, 77
Maria as "First Woman in the Republic," 2, 31, 62
Maria's articles, 30–32
Maria's editorials, reprinted, 46
Maria's tribute to, 78, xxii
May, Reverend Samuel, 32–33
moderate abolitionists, 70
pacifist beliefs, 24
picture, illus. p4
radical abolitionist, xiv
religion and moral answers, 23
slavery as moral question, 23
Thoughts on African Colonization, 23, 32
threats on life, 33–34
women's self-determination, 30
Genius of Universal Emancipation, The (Garrison), 30
Georgia, 19, 27, xiv
Greeley, Horace, 67, 69
Grimke, Angelina, 42
Grimke, Sarah, 42

H

Hancock, John, 2
Harper's Ferry, 66
Hemings, Sally, 2
Herald of Freedom, The, 62

Hicksite Friends, 56
Higginson, Thomas Wentworth, 13, xxv
"Hints to People of Moderate Fortune" (Child), 30
History of the Condition of Women, Authentic Anecdotes of American Slavery (Child), 39, 63, xvii, xxi
Hobomok, a Tale of Early Times (Child), 11–12, xv, xx, illus. p1
Hopper, Isaac and Hannah, 46, 56
Hopper, John, 46–49, 55

I

Illinois, 19, 40
immigrants
    European, xviii
    Irish, 75, xviii
    Italian, xviii
    Jewish, xviii
    Latin American, xviii
    poor, 28
Incidents in the Life of a Slave Girl (Jacobs), 71, xvi, xxii
Independent, xxii
Indian Congress, illus. p7
"Indian Wife, The" (Child), xx
Indians. *See* Native Americans
interracial union/marriage, 12, 27, xiv
Irish immigrants, 75, xviii
Isaac Royall estate, 2
Isaac T. Hopper: A True Life (Child), 55–56, xxi

J

Jackson, Andrew, 27–29
Jacobs, Harriet, 71, xvi, xxii
"Jan and Zaida" (Child), xxi
Jefferson, Thomas
    father of American democracy, 3
    Hemings, Sally, 2
    miscegenation, 3
    United States president, 2, xxvii
    Walker, David, 22
    white supremacist stance, 3, 22

Johnson, President Andrew, 77
"Jumbo and Zairee" (Child), 32, xx
Juvenile Miscellany magazine (Child), 5, 12–13, 25, 27, 32, 43, xv, xx, xxviii–xxix, illus. p1
Juvenile Souvenir; The (Child), xx

K

"Kansas Emigrants, The" (Child), 60, 62, xxi
Kansas/Nebraska Act, 58
Karcher, Carolyn
    abolitionist activities, 13
    anti-slavery movement, 8, 44–45
    "Appeal to the Colored Citizens of the World, An," 27
    baptism by Convers Sr., 9
    Child historian, xxvii
    Emancipator, 45
    First Settlers of New England, The, 27
    First Woman in the Republic, The, xxvii
    Garrison's admiration of Maria Child, 32
    interracial marriage, 27
    Juvenile Miscellany magazine, 12–13
    literary fame, 12
    Loring, Ellis, 36–37
    Lydia's mother's death, 5
    marriage of David and Maria Child, 27
    Native American rights, 13
    Quakerism, 41
    Swedenborgianism, 8
    Transcendentalism, 36–37
    Turner, Nat, 25
    women's rights, 13, 44–45
Kelley, Abby, 43–44
Kenschaft, Lori
    Child's major causes, xxviii
    law of coverture, 16
    Lydia Maria Child: The Quest for Racial Justice, 87, xxviii
    women and financial control, 62–63

L

labor unionism, 28
Lafayette, General, 14
"Letters from New York" (Child), 51, xxi
Liberator (newspaper), 24, 32–34, 46, 77
Liberty Bell (publication), xxi
Lincoln, President Abraham, 71, 73, 76, xxii
Little Girl's Own Book, The (Child), 21, xx
"Lone Indian, The" (Child), xx
Looking Toward Sunset (Child), xxii
Loring, Ellis, 36–37, 46–47, 50, 64
Louisiana Purchase, 19–20
Lovejoy, Reverend Elijah, 40
Lowell, James Russell, 36, 51
Ludlow, Reverend Henry, 79
Lydia. *See* Francis, Lydia Maria
Lydia Maria Child: The Quest for Racial Justice (Kenschaft), 87, xxviii
Lydia Maria Child Selected Letters 1817-1880 (Meltzer), 83, 87, xxvi

M

Maine, 7, 19–20, xiii
Maria. *See* Child, Lydia Maria
Martial Law, illus. p16
Mason, Mrs. Margarita, 67–68
Mason, Senator James, 67
Massachusetts, 2
Massachusetts General Colored Association, 20
Massachusetts Journal, 14, 27, 29–30, xx
May, Reverend Samuel, 32–33
Medford (Massachusetts), 1–2, 5, 54, 60, xiii
Meltzer, Milton, 83, 87, xxvi–xxvii
Mercer, Charles Fenton, 17
Milton, John, 7
miscegenation, 3
Miscegenation Ball, illus. p20
Miscellany. *See Juvenile Miscellany* magazine (Child)
Mississippi, 19
Missouri, 19–20, 58, 65

Missouri Controversy, 20
Mohammedan, xvii
monks and nuns, illus. p13
Moore, John, 20
Moral Lessons in Verse (Child), xx
Mother's Book, The (Child), 21, 35, xv, xx
Mott, Lucretia, 42, 63
"My Mother's Grave" (Child), 5
myth of African inferiority, 25, xiv

N

NASS. *See National Anti-Slavery Standard* (NASS)
National Anti-Slavery Standard (NASS), 51, xvi, xviii, xxi
National Era, 55
National Historical Publications Commission, xvi
Native Americans
  assimilation of, 11, 25, 27
  democracy without, 29
  Indian Congress, illus. p7
  integration of, xxviii
  oppression of, 4
  removal program, 29
  rights, 13
Negro exodus, illus. p16
New England Anti-Slavery Society, 32
New England Federalists, 17
New Flower for Children, A (Child), xxi
New Orleans, 39
New York Courier, 46
New York Draft Riots, 75, illus. p22
New York Tribune, 60, 67, xxi
North American Review magazine, 12, 34
Northern Republicans, 71

O

Oasis, The (Child), 43, xxi
Oberlin College, 7
Osgood, Lucy and Mary, 60
Over the River and Through the Woods to Grandmother's House We Go (song), 63, xxv

P

Paradise Lost (Milton), 7
Patriarchal Institution (Child), 70
penitentiaries and prisons, xviii
Pennsylvania, 2
Phillips, Wendell, 46
Philosophy and *Consistency* (Child), 30
Philothea (Child), 36, xxi
Plains Indians, xiv
plantation land distribution, xvi
"Plea for the Indian, A" (Child), xxii
Poe, Edgar Allen, 51
Politeness (Child), 30
Poor Richard's Almanac (Franklin), 31
post office, attack on, illus. p6
poverty, 81, xviii, xix
Preston, Mary, 5, 7, 15
prison incarceration, xix
prison system, xviii
Progress of Religious Ideas, Through Successive Ages, The (Child), 56–57, xvii, xxi
proslavers of North, illus. p8
Puritans, 28, 41

Q

"Quadroons, The" (Child), xxi

R

racial
   assimilation, 28
   bigotry, 57
   discrimination, xxvi
   equality, 34, xvi, xix, xxvi, xxvii
   prejudice, xiv, xv
   tolerance, 11
Rebels, A Tale of The Revolution, The (Francis), 14
Rebels, or Boston before the Revolution (1825), *The* (Child), xv, xx
Reconstruction Policy, 78
Redcoat, 2
religious bigotry, xix
Remond, Sarah Parker, illus. p14

Republican Congress, 77
Republican Restrictionsits, 19
"Resemblance between the Buddhist and Catholic Religions" (Child), xxii
Rhode Island, 2
Romance of the Republic, A (Child), xvi, xxii
runaway slaves, 53–54

S

school segregation, xxvi
Scott, Dred, illus. p17
Secret Six, 66, 69
Seward, William, 58–60, 71
sexist stereotypes, xix
sexual brutality, 71
sexual equality, 31
sexual exploitation, xix
Shaw, Colonel Robert Gould, 74–75, illus. p23
Shaw, Frances, 48–49
Shaw, Robert, 63
Shaw, Sarah, 63
slave(s)
   African, 1
   catching, 57
   emancipation of, 5, 34, 42, 44, 73, 75
   forced breeding, 19
   manumitted, 20
   oppression of, 52
   punishment, illus. p5
   rape by owners, 19
   rebellion, illus. p7
   runaway, 46
   three-fifths slave clause, 17
   trade, ban on transatlantic, 19
slavery
   Biblical sanctioned, 57
   British West Indies, 38
   District of Columbia, 23, 33–34
   expansion of, 28, 58
   as free market economy, 18
   in Kansas, 58
   in Missouri, 19

moral repulsion of, 58
southern, xviii
States that abolished, 2
"Slavery's Pleasant Home" (Child), xxi
"Song for the Free Soil Men" (Child), 60, xxi
South Carolina, 13, 19, 42, 58, 71
Southern Democratic Party, 58
"St. Domingo Orphans, The" (Child), 32, xx
Standard (newspaper), 45–46, 49, xviii, xxii, xxix
Stearns, George Luther, 66
Sumner, Senator Charles, 58–59, 65, 69, 77, illus. p15
Swedenborg, Emanuel, 8
Swedenborgianism, 8

T
Tallmadge, James, 19
Texas, 53
Thanksgiving Day poem (Child), 63, xxv
"The Rival Bothers" (Child), xx
13th Amendment, 76
Thompson, George, 38–39, illus. p9
Thoughts on African Colonization or *An Impartial Exhibition of the Doctrines, Principles, and Purposes* (Garrison), 23, 32
three-fifths slave clause, 17
Ticknor, George, 12, 14, 35
tolerance, 11, 27, 57, xix, xxvi, xxvii
Transcendentalism, 36–37, 47
Transcendentalist, 5, 36
Tremont Temple, 69
Turner, Nat, 24–25, illus. p7
Tyler, John, 20

U
Uncle Tom's Cabin (Beecher Stowe), 9
unequal marriages, xix
University of Massachusetts, xxvii
urban poverty, xviii
U.S. Congress, illus. p29–30

V
violence, 26, 44, 60, 68, xix. *See also* Brown, John; Civil War; Virginia insurrection; Year of the Mob
Virginia, 24, 66–67, 70
Virginia insurrection, 24–28
Virginian Press, 67

W
Walker, David, 21–22, 24–25, xviii
Wampanoag Indians, 12
Wayland Public Library (Massachusetts), xxviii
"What is Beauty?" (Child), 47
white Americans' prejudice, xv
White Lowell, Maria, 48–49
Whittier, John Greenleaf, 32
Wise, Governor Henry, 66
Woman's Advocate, xxii
Woman's Journal, xxii
women's
　abolitionist movement, 39
　control of finances, 62–63
　equal rights with men, 37, 39–40, 62, xxviii, xxix
　liberation, xvii
　oppression, 4
　rights, 13, 44–45
　role model, 37, 39
　roles in society, 11
　self-determination, 30
　self-determination of, 30
　sexuality, xvii
　suffrage movement, 37, 60, 63, 66, xvii, xxix
Worcester, Thomas, 8
Wright, Frances, 30–31
www.overtherivermovie.com, viii

Y
Year of the Mob, 38–40